All You Need Is More Love
and 101 More Musings, Essays, and Sundry Pieces

ALSO BY ROBERT LEE HILL

PROSE

*Life's Too Short for Anything but Love …
and 101 Other Musings, Essays, and Sundry Pieces*

*The Color of Sabbath:
Proclamations & Prayers for New Beginnings*

*Empowering Congregations:
Successful Strategies for 21st Century Leadership*
(with Denton L. Roberts)

*We Make the Road by Walking:
Proclamations & Prayers*

Made Whole by Broken Bread

POETRY

Hard to Tell: A Congregation of Poems, 1990-2003

All You Need Is More Love

and 101 More Musings, Essays, and Sundry Pieces

Robert Lee Hill

Kansas City

© 2019 Robert Lee Hill, All Rights Reserved

Published by Caroline Street Press
Kansas City, MO

Cover design and book interior by Jason McIntyre
Original cover typography by Sonja Shaffer

All rights reserved. This book, or parts thereof, may not be reproduced in any form without written permission from the publisher or author, except for the inclusion of brief passages in a review.

Hill, Robert Lee
All You Need Is More Love: and 101 More Musings, Essays, and Sundry Pieces

ISBN-13: 978-0-9965229-9-1

**IN MEMORIAM:
BENNIE LEE SMITH HILL**

Who gave the world more love
than she could ever have imagined

Table of Contents

FOREWORD i

INTRODUCTION iii

LOVE, LOVE, LOVE

All You Need Is (More) Love 3
The Capacity to Love 5
Love, Loving, Lovely 6
Love at Christmastime 7
A LOVE Campaign in NOLA (and KC!) 8

HOLY DAYS

Breather Sundays and Bridge Moments 11
Advent Is Here 13
A Time for Testimony in Advent 15
Journey to the Christmas Cradle 17
Christmas Is 18
Seymour and All Those Wreaths, Trees, Stars, and Crèches ... 20
Wondrous Treasures at Christmas 21
Lent 23
Increasing Your Hopefulness During Lent 25
Key Components of a Meaningful Lenten Season 27
Easter Is Arriving 29
Easter — What/Who Is It For? 31
Some More New Year's Resolutions 33

PRAYER & PRAYERS

Prayer 37
Praying — Everyone's Job 39
Hints of the Infinite 40

Dear God, Give Us Bread 42
A Thanksgiving Prayer 43
A Prayer for Holy Week 44

REMEMBRANCES, APPRECIATIONS, & EULOGIES

Saints 47
Celebrating Patsy Shawver 49
"Buck" O'Neil, Safe at Home 50
Eulogy for Thom Savage 52
Thanks for Bill Oldham 55
Thanks Be to God for Steve Jeffers 57
Thanks for Satchel Paige 59
Thankful for Samuel DeWitt Proctor 61
Remembering Martin 62
Gratitude for Gardner C. Taylor 65
Osip Mandelstam, Modern Psalmist 68
Mordecai Wyatt Johnson: Strategic, Visionary Hopefulness .. 69
In Appreciation of "God's Will" 71
George Tiller's Tragic Death 73
Remembering Pat McGeachy 75
Blaisdell Blessedness 79
Encomium for Michael Zedek 81
Margaret Smith — Celebration of Life 84

WHAT IT MEANS TO BE A MINISTER

A Call to Ministry 89
Reflections on Being a Pastor ... Here, Now, and With Joy! 91
Spiritual Checkup 92
God Loves the "Hilarious Giver" 94
Stewardship 96
The Gifts of Membership 98

Weddings 100
Jesus and the Crowds 102
G.R.A.C.E. 105
G.R.O.W.T.H. 106
Hands on the Table 108
Doxologies 112

20 QUESTIONS: A VOICE OF FAITH ANSWERS IN THE PUBLIC SQUARE

"What are the best and worst examples of parenting in the Bible?" 117

"What if I'm not certain about what I believe?" 118

"Does God hear the prayers of nonbelievers?" 119

"How far should Christian tolerance of other faiths go?" 120

"Where is the irony in the gospels?" 121

"What are we to make of the three versions of Jesus' 'last words'?" 122

"Do you see any prophecies that are coming true today?" ...123

"What about the rising number of 'nones,' as in people who claim no faith?" 124

"What about the sick and maimed animals in Malachi?" 125

"What does your faith say about living in the moment?" 126

"What do you think Jesus is up to?" 127

"How do I use my faith to learn to forgive?" 128

"Will fasting improve my faith life?" 129

"If you could celebrate Christmas in a different country, which would it be?" 130

"When does something in my life become a 'false god'?" 131

"Should I read sacred texts of a faith that's not my own?" ...132

"Does everyone have a guardian angel, even bad people?" .133

"Will faith and prayer finally feed all the poor?" 134

"What's your bucket list for Christians? In other words, what do you think a believer should do before they die?" 135

Big Questions at UMKC 137

LETTERS TO FAMILY IN A TIME OF TURMOIL & TORMENT

Election Eve — November 7, 2016 141

Inauguration Day — January 20, 2017 147

Independence Day — July 4, 2018 153

SUNDRIES

George Nakashima: "To go to sleep with an honest face." ... 161

The "Left Behind" Phenomenon 162

Tales from the Trail 164

Snow on Snow on Snow 166

Sharing Joy (Instead of Happiness) with Friends 168

Looking for a Sign 170

Musing About Museums 171

Jury Duty 173

Increasing Your "Up" Potential 175

In the Midst of Winter 176

Gratitude and Resolve at the Wall 178

Graciousness 180

Dreaming 181

Coming Home 183

Autumn's Raiment 185

Letter to Catherine 186

In Response to the Tragedy at Virginia Tech 188

From Agony to Agon: Responding to Charleston 191

A Statement of Commendation for "The Road to Maus" Exhibition (Sponsored by the Museum Without Walls) 194

"With hope and support, democracy will prevail." 198

LESSONS LEARNED

Kidney Stones: Tough and Deep-Truth Teachers 203
19 Things I Learned in New Orleans 206
Seven Mandates for Marriage 210
13 Lessons I Learned from Falling Off of a Bike 211
Things I Know Now That I Wish Knew Then 213

ACKNOWLEDGEMENTS 219

ABOUT THE AUTHOR 221

FOREWORD

Dr. Robert Lee Hill, my good friend and clergy colleague of more than twenty-five years, was kind enough to share his memories and reflections with us through his wonderfully written book, *All You Need is More Love*. Readers can digest these mellow musings in bed without fear that they may bring on a nervous night. In fact, I herewith declare that this book offers up frustration-free reading.

Dr. Hill writes about the heartsore and unseasonable death of his friend, Jesuit priest and former President of Rockhurst College, Thomas Savage. In doing so, he manages to somehow deny darkness any standing in his remembrances. Yes, there is in these writings an ineradicable desire to expose love to his readers.

In his meditation on the "Hilarious Giver," Dr. Hill explains in a non-offensive way that our giving should be "cheerful," which comes from the Greek word *hilaros*. This is in keeping with his upbeat writing, that God has a hearty belly-laugh of delight when he blesses us. Therefore, we should experience "the ultimate expression of faithful joy." There are few sounds that exceed the belly-laugh in curing our nation of its distress and divisions so rife in our culture today!

I hereby give Bob Hill kudos for a well-written book of memories.

I give readers of this book "you rock" kudos for having the intellectual and theological curiosity to read this weighty and witty tome.

By the way, I just finished a breathlessly big belly-laugh.

Additionally, Hill moves from the sublime to the subliminal as he writes to his nephews and niece on the weighty sociopolitical subject, The Donald Trump Presidency.

On the eve of the 2016 elections, "Uncle Bob" explains to Christopher, Nicholas, Catherine, Matthew, and Lincoln that he will be voting for Hillary Clinton. In fact, he may have explained his upcoming vote in a way that those of us who were deeply involved in the Clinton campaign should have presented to the public. Hill says, "To be sure, Hillary Clinton is an imperfect candidate." But, he goes on to say, "she hasn't been an embarrassment, a pathetic sham, a joke as a candidate."

Because I know Bob Hill on a professional and personal level, I am not at all surprised that he analyzes the chaotic state of the Republican Party as he observes the Republican Party nominee, Donald J. Trump. What Hill writes in these three in-depth letters is not so much partisan pronouncements as it is profound. Some of the nation's top Republicans have left the party for the exact same reasons that "Uncle Bob" describes.

Hopefully, "Uncle Bob's" nephews and niece will long remember his sage words written on July 4, 2018: "Democracy is hard because it is complicated. Democracy is hard because it involves compromise. Democracy is hard because it is suffused with competing visions and alternative approaches to nearly every issue engaged in public life."

Hill painstakingly informs his kin of the fragility of self-government. He goes on to describe the effects which the brazenly monocratic style of the current administration is already having on our once-revered U.S. rule of law. Trump's attacks on the pillars of U.S. democracy should cause Hill's niece and nephews' generation to not only tremble but to use this dangerous moment as a launching pad for political activism.

Bob Hill's way of impacting the children of his siblings is through the lost art of letter-writing. In a computerized world like ours, which lampoons letter writing, this book in general — and the letters from Bob to his nephews and niece in particular — should show us that communicating our thoughts through letters is a great way to pass our dreams on to the next generation.

— Rep. Emanuel Cleaver II

INTRODUCTION

The kind and generous reception of *Life's Too Short for Anything But Love ... and 101 Other Musings, Essays and Sundry Pieces* has occasioned this current book. However incredible it has seemed to me, there appears to be a yearning for another gathering of reflective pieces that seek to unite heart, mind, and soul.

And so this volume, urgently proffered to anyone seeking encouragement and hope during what too many experience as perilously discouraging and increasingly desperate times.

Some of these pieces have been shared in ecclesial and interfaith settings in Kansas City and elsewhere. Some came directly from within the "public square." Others were written in response to contemporary events and to questions in the "Voices of Faith" column of *The Kansas City Star*.

The themes, focal points, and topics contained herein are varied —

... first and foremost, love and its infinite capacity to enlarge and deepen and widen our lives;

... the blessings of snow and museums and jury duty;

... the raiment Kansas City wears every autumn;

... the gracings that come with pastoral ministry;

... the sacral rhythms and perennial consecrations of congregational life;

... the place and practice of prayer;

... lessons learned from bicycle accidents and encounters with kidney stones;

... celebrations of Will Campbell, Buck O'Neil, Thom Savage, Satchel Paige, Samuel DeWitt Proctor, Martin Luther King, Gardner C. Taylor, Osip Mandelstam, Mordecai Wyatt Johnson, and precious colleagues and friends whose exemplary lives have inspired countless admirers.

I hope and trust no one will take the emphasis on "love" and the book's title as saccharine declarations thrown out to pacify, numb, or evade the tense and tough dilemmas we each and all face daily. Nothing could be farther from the intent of this effort. I really do mean what the title avers: more love really can empower and strengthen us for truly satisfying and fulfilled lives.

In the end, if one person can be enthused to embody love more fully in his or her daily round, then this book will not have been wrought in vain.

— Bob Hill

LOVE, LOVE, LOVE

All You Need Is More Love

All You Need Is (More) Love

One little word. One tall, lanky cipher, and three small, squatty other letters, and not a guttural tone among them.

A word uttered glibly in moments that don't really deserve it. ("I just *love* your new car!")

A word that stutters on too many tongues of those who know what it feels like but cannot give expression to its reality in their lives. ("I just wanted to say that I ... I ... I ...")

A word that "makes the world go 'round." A word that the world does not yet hardly know, or know well enough, or know at all, given the ways human beings have devised to harm and hurt and ravage one another.

Today, it's a word more in need of embodiment than ever before. We could echo what John Lennon sang in his quasi-palindromic lyric from 50 years ago: "All you need is love, love is all you need." But now, let us be emphatic and declare, "All You Need Is **More** Love."

In all languages and at all times it is a noun which is neither person, place, nor thing. And yet it is also a verb, both transitive and intransitive.

It is an event that can involve physical affection, but it can happen without a single touch.

It suffuses the hearts of those who yearn to serve country and homeland and local community, and it fills the sails of those seeking the sights of other shores.

It develops, of course, in families, but also in book clubs, neighborhood associations, 1st and 2nd grade, and even in the "17th grade" (a.k.a. graduate school).

It evolves over years and happens in seconds.

It can be sung, and it can be felt; but it can never be ultimately denied.

Unto it some of the most stunning social customs have accrued. Unto it some of the most unusual historical traditions have become attached.

It goes beyond human logic and reason; it is part of God's magisterium of mysterious grace.

And yet it is as human and as daily as paying a bill, changing a diaper, setting a table, doing the laundry, or making a phone call.

It is blessing and benediction. It is mandate and magnificence. It is the disruption of each and every status quo. And it is the equilibrium to which all disruptions eventually, finally return.

It compels the most profitable day imaginable for florists, on Valentine's Day. And yet, in its essence, it cannot be packaged, purveyed, bought, sold, or compromised.

Without love, the symphony known as the human family — with its multitude of instruments — might just as well be a cacophony of clanging cymbals.

Without love, all our efforts at understanding and prediction are merely the dusty chalk marks of empty equations and paltry propositions, containing neither sound nor fury, signifying even less than nothing.

Without love, our endeavors to show ourselves righteous or pure or good or correct or proper or dutiful or triumphant are but vainglorious exercises which vanish like fog eluding our grasp.

The apostle Paul in his love hymn in I Corinthians 13 declares its powerful essence. As with the Corinthians back then, so with us now: it will change our lives and our life together in ways that can surely be called holy.

This love was at the foundation of the world, the beginning of time, the point of origin for all that is.

This love is the well of life that never runs dry.

And it is for our fruition.

It is the guiding star whose shining beauty never fails to enchant and inspire.

It is the touch of reconciliation that never fails to heal and save.

Again — at the risk of over-emphasizing, but still worth declaring because everyone in the world needs it so much — the word is ... "Love." All you need is *more* love!

The Capacity to Love

There are capacities within us that surprise with their intensity and power. When we claim these capacities we become who we were meant to be.

Sometimes these capacities are our given talents or our unique gifts, nonreplicable by others. But there is within us all a mutual capacity to love. We may be only mildly aware of it, or we may be dumbstruck and oblivious to it. But we all possess such a capacity. God made us that way.

When we become fully aware of our capacity to love, and exercise it on a consistent basis, we experience something similar to what others know uniquely in specific rarified moments — the way baseball players know when they master the capacity to hit a curveball, or a photographer knows when she captures an image just right, or an engineer knows how exactly to gauge the tonnage a bridge can bear, or a chef knows precisely which spice to add to a culinary creation and how much and when.

The ability to love is a God-given capacity which we neglect at our peril. But when we are aware of such a capacity and we practice it regularly, we begin to grow into the best that is possible within us, individually and together.

Jesus had a phrase for those moments when our human capacity for loving is fully expressed. He called it "the kingdom of God."

Love, Loving, Lovely

Love is the basis of faith and the touchstone of life. Jesus taught it and lived it. Our scriptures repeatedly intone it. Our lives daily confirm it.

It is the foundation of what it means to be a family.

It is at the heart of parenting.

It is the gist of our deepest friendships.

It is the cornerstone of all congregations.

It is the premier connection among human beings.

It is the first step along our quest to know God, and it is the ultimate move in our yearning to enjoy God's grace.

To say that we "love" someone or something or someplace reveals our ultimate loyalties and greatest commitments.

To describe what "loving" is like may be, at once, one of our hardest and most enjoyable tasks.

To say something is "lovely" is to clothe in words what is most beautiful in our lives.

We cannot use the lexicon of love enough, for such words are the keys to greater intimacy among human beings and the bridge to a deeper relationship with God.

Love is not merely a laudable recommendation; we can bet our lives on it.

Love at Christmastime

Love is naturally, powerfully, undeniably one of the candles on the Advent wreath.

Love is the ultimate spiritual currency for those who follow in the ways of the Nazarene carpenter.

Love is at the core of what it means to be human, and it is the essence of the One in whose image humanity has been made.

Love is the ethic of any just action that leads to true, lasting transformation.

Love is the power that forms and fuels the church that gathers in Christ's name.

Love is the foundation of all enduring relationships, in and out of the church.

Love — in all of its fashions and manifestations — is really what makes the world go 'round.

If we had only one theme to lift up at Christmas, love would surely be our eventual choice.

Love — share it, show it, say it, pray it, give it, live it.

There is no greater present beneath any Christmas tree or at the bottom of any Christmas stocking or between any one person and another. It is the boldest gift God gives to the world at Christmastime.

A LOVE Campaign in NOLA (and KC!)

The folks down in New Orleans, Louisiana, don't know exactly what to make of it, but they don't seem to mind that the Crescent City has been dotted with 350 red "LOVE" signs over the past couple of months.

At first no one seemed to know how the signs came to be so visible, why they had become so prevalent, or who was posting them. Still, most people responded favorably to the signs that suddenly appeared on light poles, street corners, sidewalk restaurant menu marquees, and the back windshields of cars. Some were intrigued about the motivation of those who posted the LOVE signs. Some gave themselves enthusiastically to interpreting the word "LOVE."

Nearly all were curious about the identity of the creators of what appeared to be a coordinated campaign. The conspirators have been shielded under a cloak of anonymity, by their preference. But the LOVE signs are doing the job the LOVErs intended: stimulating a lot of attention and causing a lot of conversation.

Which goes to show you the power of a single word and its impact on a community. It certainly has sparked a lot of rumination about how the word LOVE can be applied in the areas where New Orleans has experienced a rash of violent crimes.

Does anyone else think this just might be something we should try in Kansas City? Can we imagine together what might happen to our civic conversations if we began seeing LOVE signs at nearly every intersection in Greater Kansas City?

What if LOVE signs — small, unobtrusive, yet appealing signs — began popping up in our public spaces in the heart of the heart of the country? Surely such a LOVE campaign wouldn't hurt, and it just might contribute to some lively discussions and maybe even some healing.

HOLY DAYS

All You Need Is More Love

Breather Sundays and Bridge Moments

On the Church's liturgical calendar, every four or five years we encounter the occasion of a "Breather Sunday" between the delectable, overly satisfying experience of Thanksgiving's feasting and the commencement of the colorful, richly rewarding Advent emphasis in worship.

This is a "betwixt and between" Lord's Day. Many preachers, worship leaders, priests, deacons, and choir directors are glad for this "bridge" moment between the American Thanksgiving focus and the nearly universal observance of the Advent and Christmas seasons.

We all need "bridge" times, "bridge" places, "bridge" people, "bridge" events. Bridges allow us time to appreciate that which has just passed; they also let us catch our breath so as to heighten our anticipation of that which is coming in the future. Each experience – the past and the future – is allowed due, unhurried attention.

If you're approaching such a "bridge" moment, I offer the following suggestions for your pondering and potential action:

- Is it possible for you to say "Thanks" just one more time to someone close to you for all the blessings they've bestowed on your life?

- Notice the special Thanksgiving seasonal music. Despite the rarity of our singing them, the tunes usually are fairly familiar. Perhaps we remember them so easily because there are so few of them. Or perhaps they have such a warm, familiar sound because we associate them with the warm, familiar feelings we enjoy at a certain time of year. Whatever the origin of their endearment, notice the Thanksgiving music.

- Have you walked among piles of leaves lately? I highly recommend it. The leaf dust won't be that bad if you merely traipse through the golden-russet-magenta piles. (And if you'll allow yourself the joyful chance to kick through some leaves, maybe you'll also have the opportunity to notice the incomparable beauty of this year's rendition of fall.)

- Consider an Advent adventure which will occupy your time for the next four weeks leading up to Christmas. You may want to discuss this with your family or friends. A new hobby? A plan to travel to a new place, yet unexplored? A change in your holiday observance routines? A different way to decorate your home? Are your ready for an adventure?

- Have you thought about how we always and ultimately live our lives "in the red"? I'm not speaking of financial indebtedness, though that may be true for some. What I'm referring to is the overwhelming indebtedness we possess in relation to our forebears, the figures who really were part of the original Thanksgiving scene way back when, and to our parents and grandparents who are part of our scenes now.

Advent Is Here

"Advent is here." What a curious statement to make about a season which anticipates the arrival of that which is yet to come. Yet that is exactly what can be said among Christians four Sundays before Christmas, even as Advent commences a season of waiting, watching, hoping, and expecting.

Advent is marked by distinct characteristics.

Advent is a time of **anticipation**, not merely for long-desired special presents, but, most importantly, for a long-awaited Messiah. So, allow yourself some extra built-up hope this Advent season. Remember, the stronger the hope on the climb up the mountain, the more stunning the vista at the top.

Advent is, of course, an occasion for **devotion**. In the color purple (and in some cases blue) displayed throughout church sanctuaries, in the Advent wreaths lit each week during worship, in the particularly beautiful music which attends this holy season, devotion to God and compassion toward others are central themes. The traditions of our Advent observances call us to devote ourselves afresh to a closer personal communion with God and a vibrant embodiment of God's ways on earth.

Advent is always about God as a **virtuoso**. God, the virtuoso, tenders to the world the gift of a fragile and meek baby who is, at the same time, the ultimate incarnation of might and power. God, the virtuoso, inspires hope in lowly peasant shepherds, humbles the haughty and the prideful, and surprises the world with an ultimate expression of love and care.

Advent is always and ever **electrifying**... and educating, energizing, ennobling, emboldening, encouraging, enticing, enthralling, enthusing, engaging, edifying, and eye-opening.

Advent is ever and again about the **new**. New truths transform old possibilities into new realities for any one stuck in tired, worn-out ways. A new beginning on the church calendar starts us on a new journey of faith. Anticipating a newborn Christ child makes life brand-new for each child of God.

Advent is, of course, about **truth**. God tells the world a supreme truth in a baby whose birth-sounds in a hamlet called Bethlehem will resound throughout the world. Because of the truth of the Loving One, the world can begin to put away pretense and sham, masks and masquerades, duplicity and deception. In the season of Advent, God is coming to us in Christ to reveal the ultimate truths about our world and about ourselves.

May those who are on the road to Bethlehem experience the deepest and dearest Advent ever in anticipation of the deepest and dearest Christmas ever.

A Time for Testimony in Advent

"Testimony" is what John's gospel says Advent and Christmas are all about for those who receive the Christ child. Strange that a gospel that contains no nativity narrative should be so on-target about what this season is for.

When John's gospel describes John the Baptist, he also gives us our job description: "There was a man sent from God, whose name was John. He came as a witness to testify to the light, so that all might believe through him. He himself was not the light, but he came to testify to the light." And we? We have been bidden by God also to be witnesses, to testify to the light, so that all might believe through that One who is the light of the world.

Now, testimony can be greatly misunderstood. Testifying is not a superior way of being Christian. To testify does not exempt us from embodied service to the needs of the world. Along with testifying, we are still to feed the hungry, clothe the naked, comfort the afflicted, shelter the homeless, visit the imprisoned, tend to the sick.

Neither is testifying a matter of coming to God's defense as an expert witness. Nor is testifying trying to get other people to believe what we believe.

In his remarkable book *Testimony: Talking Ourselves into Being Christian*, Thomas Long declares a strong truth: "Trying to persuade other people to believe what we believe, whether it's politics, parenting, or religion, is a classic device to shore up our own uncertainty."

No, testimony and testifying involve us with something more.

Sometimes testifying can be tough. I must admit that I've grown weary of acquaintances who tell me, "Well, Rev., I really don't believe in the kind of God I see portrayed in some churches and by some so-called religious leaders."

"Well, Mr. So-and-So," I usually reply, "Fred Phelps is not a representative sample of what's best in the churches."

Lately I've had another sort of response. I say, "Tell me the kind of God you don't believe in, and I'll bet I don't believe in that kind of God, either. Then I will tell you about the God I do believe in."

The testimony to which John's gospel calls us and which is so central to Advent and Christmas is talking about God and our faith *as if we truly believe what we say we believe!*

So, this Christmas, let us speak and live as if we truly, deeply enjoyed our faith, and not as if we dreaded it. (It continues to amaze me how some Christians go around with sour expressions on their countenances, as if they had been baptized in a brine of lemon juice laced with garlic.) Let us offer our testimony to the world with such enthusiastic joy that others will know the authenticity of what we proclaim: "This is the day that the Lord has made. Let us rejoice and be glad in it" (Psalm 116:24).

It's helpful to remember that sharing testimony does not have to be grandiloquent, opulent, or rhetorically resplendent. It can be as humble and plain as a simple greeting, one person to another. And a humble, plain greeting just may be a life-saving moment. I can testify to that!

Journey to the Christmas Cradle

The journey to the Christmas cradle can be as short as 22 days and as long as 28 days, depending on the commencement of Advent four Sundays before Christmas Day, December 25. However long or short your path to Christmas, I encourage you to engage in the following practices:

- **Pray daily.** At home or away, while you're traveling, shopping, eating, working, studying, reading, entertaining, singing, or resting. Simply pray.

- **Offer at least one act of service** for the benefit of others, preferably for someone you don't know well.

- **Send a hand-written note of gratitude** to someone who has recently graced your life with kindness.

- **Treasure a favorite carol** and sing it. **Discover a new carol** and let it become a new favorite in your personal musical repertoire.

- **Share meals** regularly with those you love dearly and at least one meal with someone who may seem to be a stranger. With a discerning heart you will discover that both dear ones and strangers are simply children of God like you and, therefore, related to you by Christ's birth.

- **Invite others to worship.** Invite others to join you for worship on a regular weekly service during Advent or offer a special invitation for them to experience one of your Christmas Eve services. An invitation to experience the wonder, beauty, and inspiration available in a worship service (especially at Christmastime) is one of the greatest gifts you can ever give another human being.

Christmas Is ...

As the time approaches for Christmas to fulfill its annual appointment with our hearts and minds and calendars, I am aware of its many multi-valent meanings. In all kinds of climes (from equatorial tropics to deep freezes to stark, wind-swept deserts) and in all kinds of cultures (from hyper-consumerism to abject impoverishment) and in all kinds of circumstances (from relative peaceableness to strife-riddled, war-torn locations around the globe), the arrival of Christmas brings many different gifts.

Christmas is the recollection of a reclaimed past and the harbinger of a redeemed future.

Christmas is at once a lullaby and a "Hallelujah Chorus."

Christmas is a joy-saturated moment of ecstasy and a deeply running river of humble adoration.

Christmas is accepting that God is taking up residence in our neighborhood and allowing God to take up residence in our habits and our hearts.

Christmas is "child's play," a pleasure which all of God's children are invited to enjoy.

Christmas is an equal opportunity gracing experience and the most particularized sort of theological declaration.

Christmas is a "bi-focal" event, attracting our attention in two directions at once — to the skies for the testimony of "a multitude of the heavenly host" and to the earth where a lowly manger offers God's great gift of love to all.

Christmas is the most crassly exploited of the Christian holy days, and yet its essential mystery is never dulled.

Christmas is the subject of one spectacle after another, and yet its basic simplicity and truth can never be ultimately controlled or defined or warped.

Christmas is about a birthday party for Jesus and about the possibilities of a new birth of faith and love in each of us.

Christmas is early-arriving and late-coming in its appearance. For some of us, Christmas has already come. For others, it will occur well beyond the 25th of December.

Christmas is about God's fundamental, positive regard for the world, especially for the human creatures therein.

Christmas is a festive occasion — no matter how large or small the meal, regardless of whether a Christmas gathering happens inside or outside church walls — because "when God walks down the stairs,"* it's always time for feasting.

Christmas is a treasure-trove for the senses — our senses of sight and sound and smell and taste and touch delight in this incomparable season.

Christmas is remembering that everyone is someone's baby.

Christmas is an ancient rite and an evergreen sprout of unrepeatable wonder.

Christmas is found at the silent altar of a cathedral and in the rustling leaves of a brush arbor and within a steaming bowl of soup at the homeless shelter.

Christmas is about the fresh gift of healing coming into the world and the hopefulness of Christmas-celebrators, even when prognoses disappoint and chemo fails and surgeries prove less than satisfactory.

Christmas is when the spark of hope flares and the light of peace illumines and the blaze of joy enraptures and the flame of love warms, even in the most distressing of circumstances.

In the end, Christmas is a time to come home — to come home to God, to come home to family and friends and community and the world, to come home to one's soul and one's best self.

---

* Paul Scherer's phrase, as recollected to the author by Gardner C. Taylor. See Scherer's *Love Is a Spendthrift* (New York: Harper & Brothers, 1961), p. 17.

Seymour and All Those Wreaths, Trees, Stars, and Crèches

My friend Seymour dropped by my study at the church to say how impressed he's been by this year's holiday decorations in the sanctuary building.

"They're really bedazzling, I must say!" he reported with a smile as wide as the doorway he was leaning against. "It's always beautiful, but this year there's something extra going on, I believe."

"What do you think it is?" I asked.

"Well, there's more of everything," he responded.

"Like what?" I wondered.

Seymour gawked at me with incredulity. "You mean you haven't taken a walk around and seen it all?!"

"I think I've seen it all, at one time or another, passing through all the hallways and all the spaces in the building, but maybe I haven't paid as much attention as you have," I retorted. "Tell me what you've seen."

Thus began Seymour's roll-call recitation of what I had to admit is an overwhelming amount of beauty and wonder. "OK," he said, "there are 21 interior wreaths, 13 exterior wreaths, 2 greenery settings, 1 mantle decoration, 3 nativity/crèche sets, 1 manger carving, 2 Advent wreaths, 6 hanging baubles, 7 shining stars, and 7 Christmas trees."

"Seven Christmas trees? That can't be right."

"Yep, some may seem a bit small, but there're seven of them. Go count 'em!" Seymour replied with beaming confidence.

"No, I'll take your word for it. I'm just surprised is all. When you tally it up like that, it certainly is amazing. I'll have to give an extra-special word of thanks to Marce Ireland, Mary Reliford, Conchita Reyes, Kevin Freeman, Jeff Sidney, Pierre Walker, and Art Kent for all the hard work they did the three weeks leading up to Advent."

"Yes, I think they get an extra star in their crowns someday," Seymour said, summing up his appreciation.

"They've certainly given us some extra stars and a whole lot more!" I replied.

Wondrous Treasures at Christmas

During this year's sacred journey through the Christmas landscape, may you find ample space on your "to-do" lists and in your heart for the wondrous gifts of the season. The stores do not stock these items, and yet they would gladden the souls of all. Indeed, they are the most prized marvels among all the world's treasures.

The wondrous and precious gifts of the season? They are the presents which the God of Grace provides for every person on the face of the planet. They are the favors which the Lord of Love offers to every one of us, no matter how young or old, rich or poor, privileged or disenfranchised. They are the gifts which our Creator, Keeper, and Sustainer yearns for us to have in abundance, if we will but open our hearts.

Kindness — Receive the gifts of Kindness during this often unkind time. A thoughtful effort from a co-worker. A gentle proffering of help and tenderness from a loved one. A word of support from those who care about you most and best. A brave word or action offered with determination, even in the face of harsh cruelty. Kindness is what the Bethlehem Babe brings. Kindness is what the Savior inspires us to share.

Simplicity — Receive the Simple gifts of the season. Simple expressions of love and caring from your family and friends. Simple gestures of consideration and courtesy from strangers. Simple songs, simple words of encouragement, simple meals, simple encounters, simple deeds of compassion. Simplicity, we may say, is the center of a healthy celebration at Christmas time.

Love — Receive the gifts of Love during this sacred season. Love is what the Christ Child is all about. Love is what compels the truest Christmas spirit. In a rough-hewn manger, cast into an inhospitable world, the idea of Love takes the shape of human flesh in the Christ Child. If we are ready, it will take the shape of our lives, as well.

Joy — Receive the abounding gifts of Joy during these sacral days. The Joy of children, and the child-like glee of oldsters. The Joy that comes when we can see the delightful and the laughable in everything. The Joy that comes when we truly realize our utter dependency upon God and mutual interdependency with one another.

Peace — Receive the persistent gifts of Peace, the gifts the Prince of Peace most wants to give to a war-torn, strife-riddled, stress-saturated world. The Peace that instructs us in the alternatives to war and the blessings of pursuing them. The peace that arrives this time of year — at the end of a hard task fulfilled, within the clutch of a baby's fingers, whenever enemies decide to move beyond enemy-hood, in the sound of snow falling outside your kitchen window, deep within your soul when you contemplate how much God cares for you and everyone on the planet.

Lent

The Lenten season annually blesses Christians with an array of prompts to renew and deepen their faith.

Lent is a time for **letting loose**. So often we play the Lenten "game" of "giving up some bad, old habit for Lent." Thus, the trek between Ash Wednesday and Easter Sunday morning becomes like a solemn trudge down a ditch of drabness and over-serious piety. Surely piety can be enlivened with "taking on some good, new habit," not only for Lent but beyond Holy Week's high drama and within every moment of daily life. Letting loose offers many new possibilities — new reading programs, new exercise schedules, new social groups, new friends, a new weekly or daily study of a book of the Bible, new service projects, new experiences in private prayer, new excursions into intercessory prayer. Best of all, letting loose should entail the release of our own self-righteousness and the embrace of new-found self-worth.

Of course, Lent entails **engagement** with faith issues in light of fresh information and innovative knowledge. Lent is a special time to become engaged with your faith, with a renewed awareness of God's presence, and with your own vital concerns. Becoming engaged with faith means a holy encounter that will make each of us new people. And that's a central point of Lent, becoming new through the power of God which kindles amazing possibilities for human life.

Naming the holy in the midst of time is also and always a concern for the Lenten journey. This is what Jesus did, taking things and places and people who were considered totally unholy, without merit, and infusing them with great, holy significance. There is perhaps no more commanding challenge to Christians than this, that we proclaim with clear and unequivocal passion the blessed character of human existence, and that we treat all people accordingly.

And if there is sufficient letting loose, and adequate engagement with faith issues, and the appropriate naming of the holy in the midst of time, then the purpose of the Lenten season will be fulfilled: **transformation**. Metanoia, the Greek word for repentance/transformation, is what Jesus would repeat to person after person when they came after him seeking new life.

And we are still seeking today: to transform instances of hunger and starvation into situations of satisfaction; to transform the shadowy valleys of uncertainty, apprehension, and cynicism into the illuminated summits of trust, tranquility, and hope; to transform the ache of immaturity into the soothing pleasure of full development; to transform occasions of war into opportunities for peace; to transform unbelief into blessed assurance.

Increasing Your Hopefulness During Lent

Some suggestions for increasing hopefulness during this Lenten season:

(1) Jumpstart your imagination and stretch the possibilities of your own growth. One of the best ways to do so is to extend such an increase of imagination in the lives of others.

(2) Enact a media fast in your regular routine, once a week for three hours. Turn off the computer, cell phone, iPod, television, radio. No videos, movies, magazines, newspapers, or tabloids at the checkout stand. In doing so, you'll be cleansing your heart, mind, and soul of the destructive hopelessness which much of our media purveys.

(3) Pray the Lord's Prayer three times a day, morning, noon, and night. Pray it with your heart inclined toward what God might be saying to you. Listen for the meanings and messages that are intended for your own growth in grace. Listen specifically for how hope is held out to you in all aspects of your life. Listen carefully for Christ's hopefulness when he bequeathed the prayer to his first followers: "Our Father ... Thy kingdom come, Thy will be done, on earth as it is in heaven ... daily bread ... forgive ... lead us not into temptation ... deliver us from evil." Hope, hope and more hope!

I'm convinced that if you do these three steps, you will experience hope in new, life-transforming ways, as the following acronym suggests:

H — Holiness — There is holiness in authentic relationships. There is holiness potentially within us all since we have been made in the image of God. There is holiness in doing what Shakespeare reminds us to do: "Speak what we feel and not what we ought to say."

O — Openheartedness — There is a crying need for this quality in each of our lives and throughout the world. A new day can be dawning in each of our lives, no matter how long or short our time may be — a new day to live fully, if we will live with open hearts.

P — Power — Power is a gift that the season of Lent always offers, only it comes counterintuitively. Christ's power of humility and meekness was given over and over again to his disciples. The same power is offered to us in our day, through worship, study, service, and fellowship with one another.

E — Exciting Enthusiasm — The Christian faith is a journey to an enhanced experience of enthusiasm and excitement, ultimately resulting in joyfulness. To take God into our lives fully — *en-theos* — this is what enthusiastic faith is all about. To be excited — joyfully excited! — is what Christ always wants for those who would walk in his way.

Have a great Lent. There is hope enough for all!

Key Components of a Meaningful Lenten Season

The key components of a meaningful Lenten season are consistent, and easily apprehended. These central Lenten ingredients change shapes and forms, and they take on different emphases within the scheme of things each year. But, by and large, the two millennia preceding this year's sacred season have shown us the essential elements of useful and effective Lenten observances. Down through the ages these elements have included certain traditions, practices, and verities to enact. Consider:

Praying — Pray daily in solitude, and then weekly in the context of praise and celebration. Of all the disciplines most neglected and, at once, most needed, prayer sits at the top of the list. If you're having difficulty scheduling a regular time of prayer on a daily basis, consider praying for the benefit of a specific person or circumstance and as an expression of thanksgiving for some new grace that has come into your life.

Worshiping — Worship on a regular basis. Faith is always a team endeavor. Only rarely — such as with religious hermits — is faith a solo act. (And even then most hermits are inextricably part of a community.) Corporate worship does not merely empower an institution. Primarily, regular acts of corporate worship empower and transform the worshipers, who in turn transform their families, their friends, and the world. We all need to share with others those shining times of awe and reverence (as well as the shadowy times of vulnerability and need) which worship affords.

Practicing Hospitality — Practicing hospitality, especially with strangers, will definitely provide different perspectives on the world and within our own hearts. A word of grace, offered by you in a seemingly plain sort of occasion just might be the touch of caring that will turn someone's journey toward hope and goodness. Everyone treasures hearing the phrase, "You're welcome here."

Doing Deeds of Service — Try to proffer a little kindness each day, particularly with people you do not know well and especially with people you do not know at all. A deed of service, an action for the cause of justice, an expression of love on your part can be the very moment when someone's parched soul is slaked and satisfied. Assume everyone you meet is carrying a heavy burden.

Revisiting Prior Spiritual Commitments — All of us, at one time or another, have made special promises and pledges to God regarding the state of our religious devotion. Recall those precious moments of covenant and renew your previously held commitments for your present circumstances. The renewing of vows isn't just for special wedding anniversary celebrations. Consider what it might mean for you, your family, your friends, your congregation, if you were to renew the profession of your faith. From such renewals have come the greatest personal, societal, and global movements for goodness' sake.

One caution: If we will pray, worship, practice hospitality, serve, and renew our faith commitments during Lent or any other season, we will never be the same. And, I suspect, the world will never be the same, either.

Easter Is Arriving

Easter is arriving with a powerful message of resurrection and hope for one and all!

That's what all the festival celebrations are all about at churches across the land: emphasizing and highlighting the truths that (1) God's love can and does overcome everything and (2) hope springs eternal because of God's presence with us.

Though death may seem a terrifying, unconquerable obstacle on life's road toward meaning, God's word of eternal life renders that obstacle into a pile of powerless dust. While hatred, meanness, and injustice are witnessed daily throughout the globe, God's victorious love in Christ always has the last word.

As you approach the glorious Easter celebrations, consider the following acronym of meanings as a guide for your faith journey during this season of the church calendar:

Emerging — Easter is about emerging — sprouts from the ground, buds from tree limbs, newborn babies in the arms of glassy-eyed new parents, the risen Christ emerging from an empty tomb.

Affirming — Easter is about affirming — affirming forgiveness for a world "in sin and error pining," affirming encouragement for the struggling student, affirming sobriety for a person overcoming, one day at a time, their struggles with addiction, affirming life for any community wounded by death and degradation.

Sustaining — Easter is about sustaining — God's sustaining grace which empowers people in warn-torn countries to prevail against genocide, God's sustaining presence which empowers a hospital patient to endure in the midst of great fear, God's sustaining spirit in our hearts, within the community, and by the side of each one who walks the path of faith.

Telling — Easter is about telling, telling the exceedingly good news that "Christ is risen!," telling someone about what faith has done in your life, telling a disbelieving crowd that unmerited, free-flowing grace is the cornerstone of a life worth celebrating.

Embracing — Easter is about embracing, embracing one another in loving care, embracing the future with all of its promises, embracing the possibility of great surprises, embracing grace as it comes to everyone.

Resurrecting — Easter is, of course and always, about resurrecting, resurrecting old hopes and new dreams, resurrecting fresh, new encounters and lifelong friendships, resurrecting closer family ties and newly reconciled relationships, resurrecting good jobs for people yearning for real work and an exciting venture on a new career path.

So, let us celebrate all the emerging, affirming, sustaining, telling, embracing, and resurrecting aspects of Easter's glory.

Easter — What/Who Is It For?

"But what is Easter for?" he asked from behind some Tennessee prison bars.

"What does Easter really prove?" she sneered from across the banquet table.

"How do we know that Easter actually happened?" they wondered, as their eyes traced the fluttering of fireflies and the rising of campfire sparks into the nighttime sky.

Questions such as these come to clergy folks all the time, from both pedestrian agnostics, playful friends who like to question the basis of Christian belief, and earnest members of the Church. And always, every spring, when we climb to the bright summit of Easter Sunday's great news of God's love overcoming death, such questions rise once again.

Allow me to suggest, however, that the main question concerning Easter — "What is Easter for?" — needs to be recast in the following manner: "*Who* is Easter for?"

This is the main question to ask, since God's gift of Jesus of Nazareth was a very personal response to our very personal needs for a very personal encounter. What the world needed, and needs still today, is not merely an abstraction which might possibly elicit an intellectual engagement of our mental processes. Rather, we yearn for, we hunger for, a total (holistic) response to our deepest hungers, most particularly the deep hunger for the divine. So, let us ask, "*Who* is Easter for?"

Easter is for everyone touched by hardship and hunger —
    for the homeless child in downtown Kansas City,
    for the senior citizen whose legacy of independence is shrinking,
    for the illiterate mother of three children who works four jobs to make ends meet,
    for the struggling grandmother in the long bread line in Yugoslavia,
    for the veteran paraplegic in Cambodia,
    for the Vietnam veterans standing forlornly at our doorways,
    for the struggling students of Tiananmen Square fame,
    for the huddled masses of Honduras...

Easter is for everyone who has battled loneliness and heartache — for the business tycoon who knows the vacuity of making material things into ultimate concerns, for the widows and widowers who miss so deeply the companionship of the one they once called "beloved," for the janitor who sees no end to dirty floors, for the teacher who catches the early signs of defeatism in the dull eyes of a despairing young one, for the person racked by the painful and haunting memory of early childhood abuse, for the father who watches a son grow distant and aloof, for a grandmother who sees a granddaughter enter into the valley of the shadow of death...

Easter is for everyone who has struggled against all the odds — for the small farmer who maintains a grand vision of the family's stewardship of their small piece of earth, for the attorney who helps the great and the meek with grace and caring, for the doctors and the nurses who help countless patients do battle with disease and illness, for the secretary who holds a business together with the finesse of her personality and her quicksilver timing, for the truck driver striving to balance a financial sheet at the end of the month and not violate weight or speed restrictions, for the painter who remains vigilantly faithful to what she envisions in her imagination, for the musician who remains consonant with the inner music he hears, for the salesman who really does believe in his product and deals fairly, for the social activist who champions a cause which no one else will touch...

We could go on, but we don't need to. Simply put, Easter is for **everyone**! May God bless us, every one of us, here and everywhere, during every Easter celebration and forever.

See you in Church!

Some More New Year's Resolutions

This week, an arbitrary mark on a calendar signals that it's time to start living anew. Some will begin a new diet. Some will seek to break an old habit. Others will say, "Good, I'm glad that year is over and gone!" Still others will wonder how the New Year will be as good for them as the old year was.

In whatever circumstances you find yourself, I offer the following for your consideration as New Year's resolutions for the coming 365 days and beyond.

Walk — Do yourself a favor in the New Year and walk on a regular basis. Even if you already ride a bike or jog. The past year was a banner year in my walking experience — on the Trolley Trail, throughout our Brookside neighborhood, and down at Union Station. But I plan to experience even more walking blessings in the New Year. Resolve to give your mind, body, and spirit the peace-inducing (and healthy!) gift of walking on a regular, disciplined basis.

Break Bread with Friends-to-Be — Imagine for a moment the precious occasion of sharing an unhurried meal with a friend. Such feasts are what holiday joys and restfulness and abiding gratitude are made of. Resolve to break bread with at least one new friend-to-be each month in 2013. I'll wager a free lunch on me that you'll experience a jolt of rejuvenation to your spirit by doing so.

Share the Music — We don't have to be in the middle of Christmas to enjoy great music in connection with the church. Any time and any place will do. Resolve this year to listen to at least one new CD and one new concert and/or musical celebration that you haven't experienced before.

Listen — One of the highest compliments ever to be paid to anyone is to really listen to them. We all know the luxurious pleasure it is to be listened to, to be really, deeply heard, by a friend or even a stranger. Resolve to practice the subtle and saving art of listening in order to truly hear and understand others and stop rehearsing what you want to say.

PRAYER & PRAYERS

All You Need Is More Love

Prayer

A tragedy-riddled zone of conflict in a war-torn country ... a quiet evening at your kitchen table ... as children get out of the car and rush into school for further learning adventures ... enduring a frustrating afternoon on your job ... in your car on the way to worship on Sunday morning ... in the check-out line at the grocery store ... waiting for a plane to arrive or to leave ... at the coffee shop with a friend ... late at night, preparing for sleep, as you review the day's occurrences. What do all these occasions have in common? All of them are proper opportunities for acts of prayer.

Prayer may be viewed from a wide array of perspectives:

- as the heartbeat of religious life;
- as the main theme of spirituality;
- as the major chord in which the tone of the holy is cast;
- as the mother of all rivers of faith;
- as humanity's main access to a loving Creator;
- as the most elemental task of a Christian;
- as the bedrock of our belief system;
- as the lifeblood of the Church around the world;
- as the one absolutely essential item for proper worship.

However our views of prayer have evolved, each of us, at some point or another in our faith journeys, is eager to delve deeper into this crucial subject and learn more about improving our prayer practices.

There's no doubt that what we have to pray about will have no end. The ways and manners of our prayers, and the realities which elicit thoughtful and heartfelt prayers continue to challenge experts and novices alike.

For the time being — particularly during the Lenten season of exploration and renewal — consider the following as guides to your prayer times.

In our prayers let us offer thanksgivings galore for the wondrous events of worship that are yours to experience.

In our prayers let us also offer petitions for peace, needed so much throughout the world but particularly in the Middle East and Africa.

Let us also pray prayers of hope and encouragement for those considering becoming members here at Community.

In all our prayers let us give over to God's gracious care all our worries and anxious concerns about all matters. Challenges at our jobs, at school, in our homes, and within the wider reaches of the community can overwhelm us if we let them. Or we can simply put each challenge in proper perspective and know — deep down! — that we are taken care of wonderfully well by God's grace

Let us be vigilantly gentle with ourselves, and convey the same attitude toward others who very probably, like us, are looking for deeper understanding and broadened confidence as they progress along their faith journey with God.

Praying — Everyone's Job

Every person of faith has work to do, even if they're still in school or retired, on the job or unemployed, on vacation or simply musing through a day. Spiritually speaking, everyone has a job. The job? Praying.

To increase our awareness of prayer's goodness and graces, it's also helpful to try out some daily prayer guidelines. Thus the following suggestions:

Seven Steps for Praying as Part of Your Daily Schedule

1. Pray for the benefit of others — for those you will encounter, those you pass along the way, those who meet your gaze, and those who don't even detect your presence. Pray for justice and mercy to attend the daily paths of all people.

2. Pray for the fulfillment of your best dreams and highest hopes. Pray for the fulfillment of everyone's "calling."

3. Pray for the health of your co-workers, friends, and neighbors.

4. Pray for forgiveness for yourself and for all people.

5. Pray at least three times — a prayer of hope when beginning the tasks of your day; a prayer of gladness in the middle of the tasks; a prayer of gratitude as you finish the tasks.

6. Pray the 23rd Psalm as an affirmation of the God of your life and the God of all life.

7. Pray a rest-full prayer (sorting and assessing) at day's end.

Hints of the Infinite

From whence do you receive hints of the infinite? Surely some portion of our reflective moments is given over to consideration of those instances of what Wordsworth called "Intimations of Immortality." Surely each of us has pondered in our hearts, like Mary before Jesus' birth, messages and meanings that defied logic, calculation, and final definition. Surely we all have puzzled over the possibilities of God's mysterious presence in our daily earthly lives and what that presence will be like in the life that is to come.

In traditional Christian belief systems, most notions about the numinous netherworld beyond earthly life are summed up with the term "heaven." In fact, throughout the vast span of Christian heritage, so much emphasis has been placed on the importance of a human reckoning with "heaven" that other items of equal importance, at least from the perspective of Jesus' proclamations in the Bible, have been paid little attention. Too often, the Church has been guilty of promulgating a "pie-in-the-sky" theology to the entire neglect of the poor and oppressed whom Jesus so obviously called his followers to serve. For too many Christians, their hearts, minds, and souls were so thoroughly otherworldly-focused that their faith was really no earthly good.

And yet, and yet ... I believe that we also find in the course of our religious journeys that a concentration on the spiritual dimensions of our lives is the ultimate source of inspiration and nourishment for the doing of our faith. I have witnessed countless well-intentioned individuals and groups who were firmly rooted in service to others and commitments to justice and compassion who eventually burned out and forsook their service and commitments. Their roots went only so deep, and they couldn't stand the pressures which their activism brought to bear on their families, their colleagues, and their personal lives.

When we survey the practices and habits of stellar religious leaders, we discover how important a "heavenly" focus shapes their struggles and triumphs with a defining purpose and refining power. Time and again devotions, daily prayers, rituals and routines of focusing on that which we understand to be holy has provided the very energy necessary for our religious heroes and heroines to do their crucially needed, always difficult, seemingly impossible work.

The leaders of the Southern Christian Leadership Conference who helped to transform the civil rights landscape of the United States consistently knelt in prayer before major public actions.

Mother Theresa and her followers say the prayers of their daily office without fail between appointments to tend the dying and ministering to the so-called "untouchables" of India.

Cardinal Joseph Bernardin could not have as "victorious" an encounter with cancer without the prayers of countless thousands who stood in awe of his faithful witness.

Tony Campolo believed God's powerful presence in the daily practice of prayer is more important than preaching or hearing ten thousand sermons.

God is the Master Designer of *all* the world. From the perspective of faith we can aver with fervor and undaunted conviction that finally there really is no such thing as "other-worldliness." God is our Creator, the loving Maker, Redeemer, and Sustainer of one cosmos, which has many dimensions, some of them quite mysterious and baffling.

Dear God, Give Us Bread

Dear God, give us bread today.

Guide us to seek the right bread, the good bread. Help us to find the true bread which can satisfy all our appetites.

If we are merely busy with the bread of idleness, give us the bread of purpose and fulfillment.

If we are fed up with the stale crumbs of loneliness, give us the fresh taste of togetherness and friendship.

If we are malnourished because of our overly steady diet of the bitter bread of enmity, provide for us the sweetness of the bread of peace and calming love.

If we are yearning for the bread of domination, inspire us to consider instead the bread of cooperation.

Fill us, dear God, with the bounty from your hands of grace and your heart of love, and then send us out to all our hungry neighbors so that they might share in the same bread —

the bread of gladness,

the bread of wholeness,

the bread of love,

the bread which you give us through Christ Jesus, the very Bread of Life — in whose name we pray.

AMEN.

A Thanksgiving Prayer

This Thanksgiving Prayer is offered for common use, individually and among families and friends, for Thanksgiving meals wherever you may gather. Alongside the situations that challenge us to new expressions of courage and dedication, we still have so much for which to be thankful.

God of one and God of all,
we pray Your holy blessing
   on those who gather with gratitude
     around thanksgiving tables,
here and everywhere,
   families reunited
     and friends made welcome and glad.

For Your provision,
   prodigal in its abundance,
we are thankful.

For the life we enjoy
   and the living we would dare,
we are thankful.

For the hopes engendered,
   here and beyond,
we are thankful.

And we remain grateful still
for yet more blessings:
   Your strength among us;
   Your love within us;
   Your peace when we pray and when we play,
     in our work and in our rest,
     in our dreams and in our jests.

With deep thanksgiving, then,
   we pray for Your lasting,
     shining *shalom* on all this day. Amen.

A Prayer for Holy Week

Gracious and Loving God,
    as a river seeks the ocean,
    as night rises to day,
    as birds reach for the sky,
    as children yearn for nurture and acceptance,
    as parents seek out the wisdom of ancestors,
so we seek Your presence, Your eternal grace,
and Your saving, redeeming power.

We praise Your holy name —
    a name above all divisions,
    a name beyond all differences,
    a name that unites apart from all disloyalties,
    a name that beckons us to glory.

We give You thanks for the life we share together in the spirit of Christ,
whose journey in his last week of earthly life
gives encouragement and grace to one and all.
Lead us by Your kindly light that we might know better
the paths we should go.

Guide us by Your deep love that we might know that …
    the answer to worry is hope,
      (which is the best use of imagination);
    the answer to hate is love of neighbor
      (which is the best use of passion);
    the answer to confusion is truth
      (which is the best use of intellect).

Create in each one of us — each and every day
but especially this Holy Week —
a clean heart, a ready mind,
a peaceful soul, and an eager will
to be Your people after the example of Christ. AMEN.

REMEMBRANCES, APPRECIATIONS, & EULOGIES

All You Need Is More Love

Saints

In modern times, the word "saint" has become tainted with a kind of perfectionism. When many folks call someone a saint they seem to mean that the person they're describing is a kind of "Super Holy Person," above reproach and beyond correction of any kind. Then there are cynical folks who abide in the attitude of Ambrose Bierce and chuckle as they describe a saint as "a sinner, revised and edited."

The term "saints" was used by the earliest followers of Jesus simply to describe Christian believers. This is its usage in the New Testament and in the earliest extra-Biblical historical works that give testimony to the Church's development.

The apostle Paul has a particular affinity for the term "saints," using it more often than all the other New Testament writers combined.

On or near the first Sunday of November, Christians across the land celebrate "All Saints Sunday" with an eye toward the earliest understanding of the "saints" terminology. When the names and the faithful witness of those who have gone before us this past year are read in the midst of an "All Saints" moment, the inheritors of their legacies honor the contributions they made among the long line of saints who have contributed to the progress of every congregation that has ever existed.

As you approach the momentous occasion of All Saints Day or All Saints Sunday, remember to bless one and all, recalling with gratitude how we have been abundantly graced by the saints who have passed among us. May some of our blessings include the following...

- Blessings on those who are joyous in their faith, who take God seriously but themselves less so, who laugh at the divine comedy which is human existence.

- Blessings on those who are kind to the vulnerable, patient with the harsh, and abiding in their prayers for all.

- Blessings on those who never are fully aware of their talents and yet who share those talents with grace, style, and humility.

- Blessings on those who are steady in their service, always pulling their own weight and the loads of many others.

- Blessings on those who live out their relationships in the family tree of the Church, sometimes as aunts, sometimes as grandfathers, sometimes as nephews, sometimes as mothers, and always as brothers and sisters.

- Blessings on those who dare to live lives of pizzazz and power and who never doubt God's presence day by day.

- Blessings on those who are wise enough to let others believe for them when their own faith has grown dim and thin, who know first-hand what spiritual resurrection means.

Celebrating Patsy Shawver

When Village Presbyterian Church, in Prairie Village, Kansas, was celebrating its 50th anniversary in 1999, the members of that stellar congregation made a daring and visionary move by reaching across state, economic, and racial lines of normative demarcation to establish the Front Porch Alliance.

Of course, they had cake and books of memorabilia to mark their festivities, but their final focus was not on the past but on the future and what they could do to witness to their faith.

Located in the Ivanhoe neighborhood of Kansas City, Missouri, Front Porch Alliance has done extraordinary work in the areas of neighborhood betterment, tutoring and mentoring for young people, job assistance, and neighborly advocacy for the past 13 years.

At the helm of FPA's endeavors since its inception has been Executive Director Patsy Shawver. The choice of Patsy to fill that position was a natural and easy one to make, simply because she had displayed a lifelong commitment to community involvement. At FPA she blossomed even further.

I've known Patsy for longer than she's been at FPA, and it was a privilege and an honor to serve as the emcee for the tribute celebration held for her on Sunday, November 18, at the Mohart Center on the occasion of her retirement from FPA.

Village Presbyterian Church could have had no better representative or witness to the gospel's call to service and compassion than Patsy. Her beaming smile, genuine caring, enthusiasm for life, keen intelligence, and abiding spirit of mutuality with all people at all times are gifts that leave her friends inspired and humbled all at once.

Patsy has shown us what it means to bear the love of Jesus in the world. She bequeaths to FPA and the Ivanhoe neighborhood a grand legacy of lives transformed and relationships renewed. To the FPA Board of Directors she leaves some huge shoes to fill.

"Buck" O'Neil, Safe at Home

"Buck" O'Neil is now safe at home. Which is to say that we can give God thanks for a man who gave so much to others and who is now, after nearly 95 years of earthly life, at rest and complete peace with God in a dimension we can only dream of.

Buck O'Neil's passing will surely leave a hole in Kansas City's civic life no one else can fill. His life and legacy have been well documented and will be remembered with gladness at his public memorial service at Memorial Auditorium.

He was associated with the Kansas City Monarchs, as a player and later as a manager, for the majority of his career in the Negro Leagues. He twice won Negro League batting titles (1940 and 1946). In every Negro League All-Star game in which he managed (four in all), his teams were victorious.

He interrupted his baseball career to serve in the U.S. Navy in 1944-45.

His intelligence as a ball player, his savvy as a manager, and his passion for the game itself endeared him to countless fans and to numberless folks who didn't know much about baseball except through "Buck."

He helped to send more Negro League baseball players to the previously all-white Major Leagues than any man in baseball history. Among those he assisted were legendary players like Ernie Banks, Elston Howard, and Satchel Paige.

He broke the color barrier for baseball scouts in 1956, when he became a scout for the Chicago Cubs.

In 1962 he broke the color barrier for coaches in the Major Leagues, when he became a coach for the Cubs. He would go on to discover superstars like Joe Carter and Lou Brock.

In his later years, he chaired the Negro Leagues Baseball Museum Board of the Directors and served on the Veterans' Committee of the National Baseball Hall of Fame.

He was prominently featured in Ken Burns's *Baseball* documentary on PBS in 1994 and thereafter became a national icon. His tireless efforts to keep the history of the Negro Leagues alive resulted in one of the marquee public venues in Kansas City, the Negro Leagues Museum in the 18th and Vine district.

Perhaps most prominent among the memories which Kansas Citians will treasure about "Ol' Buck," as he liked to call himself in his twilight years, was his constant spirit of hope-filled joy, plainly seen and ever-present in his radiant smile.

Countless churches and civic groups all around the greater Kansas City metropolis will continue to treasure how he graced a pulpit or a fellowship hall. And Kansas Citians will continue to learn what graciousness is all about as we recollect how he handled the denial of his entrance into baseball's Hall of Fame in Cooperstown. He was, as he described how he wanted to be remembered, "a fellow who lived a life he loved living and who died always learning about people."

His love of life and his refusal to drink from any cup of bitterness are lasting gifts to be treasured and emulated, until we, too, are "safe at home."

Eulogy for Thom Savage

He was a prince. As a priest, as a pastor, as a professor, as a college president, as a proponent of civic betterment, but most of all as a friend, he was a prince. Yes, simply a prince of a man. To paraphrase Shakespeare, we won't see the likes of such royalty again for quite some time. Many hearts will remain wounded for a good while because of the great love and affection and respect we shared for this prince of a man. Beyond all the accolades and public acclaim we might muster for him, this prince was our friend, a friend extraordinaire.

Father Thom Savage died peacefully, on Monday afternoon, May 10, surrounded by the comfort of family and friends, in the geographical and spiritual bosom of his priestly order, the Society of Jesus, at the Jesuit Campion Residence and Renewal Center in Weston, Massachusetts. On Friday, May 14, a funeral service was held in the Campion Center's Chapel of the Holy Spirit, and his earthly remains were laid to rest on the grounds there, with great dignity and love, amidst a day of warm grace and sunshine, a day which one might have appropriately called a perfect "Thom" day.

Thom exhibited his princely character wherever he was and wherever he went: in corporate boardrooms all across the United States; among non-profit organizations like our own local endeavors of the Kaufman Foundation and Menninger Clinic; in a college cafeteria with eager students seeking knowledge and wisdom; around the console of radio program studio; raising money for a long list of favorite causes; riding his bicycle along the beautiful boulevards of Kansas City; dancing his heart out with passion; counseling a godson about pathways toward fulfillment and a better future.

Thom and I knew each other as acquaintances in the community prior to 1993, but we, together with Rabbi Michael Zedek, came to be a trio of friends through *Religion on the Line*, the now renowned weekly radio call-in show on KCMO 710AM, which we co-anchored with Michael each Sunday for more than five years. With an ironic yet poignant touch of timing, Thom died the day after *Religion on the Line* celebrated its 6th anniversary, on Mother's Day. I think it is safe to say that both Michael and I and the audience in radio-land knew that Thom best embodied a sterling quote by Pope John XXIII, a quote which would become our show's motto: "Let us look at each other without mistrust. Let us meet each other without fear. Let us talk with each other without surrendering principle."

When I learned of his death, I recollected Thom's unflinching and joy-filled faith as a Catholic. Then and now I cannot think of anyone who has ever, publicly or privately, challenged my Protestantism as fervently as Thom did. And I know that no one has ever respected it more. He was catholic in the "universal" sense of the word: universal in his approach to faith, as an academician, in his advocacy for universal access to the goods and justices which our society can convey to its citizens, with a universal sensitivity as a city planner and a civic dreamer. He was a priest in the best and oldest senses of the Latin word — *pontifex* — a "bridge builder" between rich and poor, insiders and outsiders, Catholics and Protestants, Jews and Gentiles, Kansas Citians and the World, the sweet and the sour, the good, the bad, and the ugly, the better, the best, and the beautiful among us.

Thom's combination of brilliant intellect, undying compassion, and seemingly indefatigable spirit were and will remain rare. And how we will cherish the memories! Memories of ...

- One who — because of his enthusiasm, joy, and sense of wonder — could always provide us with answers to our toughest questions, and conversely, would also gladly provide us with his toughest questions to all of our answers.

- One who had such difficulty breathing but still was himself such a breath of fresh air to all.

- One who was peripatetic to the nth degree with all of his wanderings, and who helped us all to settle down in our communities, in our cities, in our educational pursuits, in our organizations, and in churches, temples, and synagogues.

- One who was not allowed the blessing of counting the years, but who blessed us all by making his years count.

May Thom's favorite prayer, which was originally authored by a fellow Jesuit, Fr. Pedro Arrupe, be ours: "More than ever I find myself in the hands of God. This is what I have wanted all my life from my youth. But now there is a difference; the Initiative is entirely with God. It is indeed a profound spiritual experience to know and feel myself so totally in God's hands."

Thanks for Bill Oldham

William E. Oldham, Choral Director of Community Christian Church in Kansas City, Missouri, for 34 years, passed away on Saturday, May 13, 2006. His sudden death, due to a heart attack, shocked his family and friends, including Community's membership, and the wide array of musical associates Bill has known throughout his life in the greater Kansas City area, throughout the nation, and around the world.

During Bill's 34 years at Community, members and friends were treated to his talent, his enthusiasm, and his inimitable style of coordinating and conducting our music program, particularly the Chancel Choir's efforts during the 10:30 a.m. service.

Worshipers at Community were the beneficiaries of his energized efforts on Sunday mornings, as he inspired praises to God to symphonic levels of exultation.

Hearts were both softened and emboldened by *pianissimo* tones in 34 years' worth of Maundy Thursdays. Under his consistent tutelage and inimitable cajoling, the members of the Chancel Choir offered their glorious *fortissimo* proclamations on special Christmas Music Sundays and Holy Week Sundays over the course of four decades.

Countless thousands were brought closer to the spiritual experience of "the music of the spheres," as Maltbie D. Babcock called it, by what Bill Oldham's charges have performed in our midst.

Bill's devotion to music in general and to Community's music program, specifically, was impressive, statistically, relationally, and artistically. Gratitude runs deep for: the countless trips Bill made to and from church (for choir practice, worship, department and committee meetings, and special church events); his arranging, coordinating, and overseeing the music portions of worship services; his assisting at funerals, memorial services and weddings; his supervision of the development of singers into mature musicians and better Christians; his participation as part of the church staff team.

I was personally and pastorally grateful for Bill's faithfulness over the years, as I recall how he participated in the earnest strivings of Community's family of faith in the midst of great social changes (during his earliest years), maintained a vigilant commitment to excellence and faithfulness (during his middle years with us), and enhanced our experience of victorious celebration (during his more recent years with us).

How precious are the memories of shared life with Bill: a favorite anthem that the choir would offer during a Sunday morning service; the unique way he had of encouraging excellence from choir members; his laugh at a funny situation or scenario; sharing grief over the death of his and Barbara's son Kevin Oldham and the celebration of Kevin's wondrous music on Easter weekend, 1993; his big-hearted spirit; his culinary talents; his undying love of music, and church, and life, and — most especially — his family.

For all that Bill has seen and heard, for all that we have seen and heard because of his gifts and graces, let us say thanks be to God.

Thanks Be to God for Steve Jeffers

As we all know, and as some know all too well, Steve Jeffers's death leaves unimaginable holes in the hearts of his family, especially his wife Jan, and a gaping, gasping absence here among the family of care at Shawnee Mission Medical Center and in the network of relations and connections that make up the Institute for Spirituality in Health. The shock of his passing lingered then and still lingers now. Such is our human response when affections are so profound and a departure is so sudden.

I first came to know the dearness of Steve's friendship through clergy gatherings around the greater Kansas City area and in discussion groups connected to the Center for Practical Bioethics (formerly the Midwest Bioethics Center). Like so many of you, I always experienced Steve's phone calls and cheery e-mails as welcome blessings. In recent years it was a special grace to see the growing work of the Institute for Spirituality in Health, and I count it a singular privilege to have been involved in the pioneering physician-clergy group Steve convened at SMMC. (He was the only person ever able to get me up for a 7:00 a.m. meeting for such heady discussions.)

In the wake of Steve's passing, shock and disbelief will continue for a good while, for, because of the depth of our respect and the length of our love, we are not yet ready to let him go.

Steve was a rare combination of gifts and graces:

- He was a complicated man with a simple style.

- He was a "people person" of the first rank — eager to greet each and all with a smile — but at ease in the solitary task of writing books.

- His desk was always straightened and carefully arranged — indicating, for my taste, a bit of compulsion! — but he always allowed his soul to be rearranged and reconfigured for the needs of others.

- He was equally passionate in relation to the Seminoles at his beloved alma mater, Florida State University, and about the prodigious and important work he was completing on a "Physicians' Desk Reference on Spirituality."

- He was equally enthusiastic about cruising along on a motorcycle and investigating the ethical intricacies of neo-natal complications.

- He had been a boisterous Baptist — and a Baptist preacher to boot — but he gladly became a devoted Disciple of Christ.

- His brow could scrunch up in a fevered earnestness and yet he laughed like a fun-loving child.

- He was an early riser but he was not unacquainted with the dark night of the soul.

- He could tell really bad, corny jokes but there was nothing cornball about his abiding respect for others, especially those with whom he worked most closely.

- He was an ardent Christian whose heart was so full of the love of God that there was simply no room in it for disdain or disrespect or dismissiveness toward those who walked other religious paths. Instead there was in Steve only grace and welcome and an openness that can only be described by the word "holy."

Steve Jeffers, who taught so many people in so many ways and in so many places about death and dying, never really prepared us for his own death. But then again, how could he, how could anyone? And yet, in his exuberant embrace of life in all of its beauty, intrigue, and splendor, Steve fully embodied the truth of a saving aphorism: "We don't beat the grim reaper by living longer but by living well."

(Offered during a Memorial Service on August 20, 2008, at Shawnee Mission Medical Center.)

Thanks for Satchel Paige

As you receive these reminders of Satchel Paige's "Six Rules for How to Stay Young" and the parallel ways to stay civil, know that you can also behold Satchel Paige's actual grave marker (including the chiseled declaration of the six rules) in Forest Hill cemetery on Troost Ave., right here in Kansas City, Missouri.

From the day of his birth, July 7, 1906, to the day of his death, June 6, 1982, Satchel Paige was always young.

Satchel Paige garnered legendary status throughout his 22 years in the Negro Leagues and, after 1948, during 18 more years in the integrated major leagues.

In 1948 he entered the majors at the age of 42, the oldest rookie in the history of the game.

It was estimated that over his career he pitched in 2,500 games, played for 250 teams (the Kansas City Monarchs principal among them), and threw 100 no-hitters.

In 1965, at the age of 59, Satchel Paige started a game for the Kansas City A's (went three innings, gave up a hit and got a strikeout).

I give thanks to God for Satchel Paige's great prowess, which led him to be inducted into baseball's Hall of Fame in Cooperstown in 1971. But I give even more thanks for his inspiring wisdom.

"How to Stay Young," by Satchel Paige

1. Avoid fried meats which angry up the blood.
2. If your stomach disputes you, lie down and pacify it with cool thoughts.
3. Keep the juices flowing by jangling around gently as you move.
4. Go very lightly on the vices such as carrying on in society. The social ramble ain't restful.
5. Avoid running at all times.
6. Don't look back. Something might be gaining on you.

"How to Stay Civil" — adapted after **Satchel Paige**

1. Avoid fried meats and fried radio call-in show hosts which angry up the blood.
2. If your stomach or an adversary disputes you, lie down and pacify them with cool and calm thoughts.
3. Keep the juices for justice flowing by jangling around gently with fairness as you move among everyone.
4. Go very lightly on the vices, church, such as pride. Just as the social ramble ain't restful, the praise of the world doesn't lead to ultimate peace.
5. Avoid running and panicking at all times.
6. Don't look back, except to learn from the past. Santayana's wisdom remains indisputable: Those who do not learn from the past are condemned to repeat it. And if we do learn from the past, then we need never fear anyone or anything that might be gaining on us.

Thankful for Samuel DeWitt Proctor

Some souls enter space and time with such effervescence and power, with such quintessential distinction and impact that, after their earthly ships have steered toward their final harbors, their wake touches shoreline after shoreline with hardly any indication of ceasing. Such a soul was and is Samuel DeWitt Proctor.

To review Proctor's astonishing career is to witness someone with a high purpose and in a hurry. A high school graduate at age 15, a college president at age 34, Proctor was always sought for his wisdom and wit, his keen intelligence and spiritual insights. He was twice a college president, thrice a congregational pastor, thrice a professor, and four times engaged in endeavors for social transformation initiated by agencies of the U.S. government.

His academic credentials and effectiveness (particularly in the area of improving education for minorities) were surpassed by the "street cred" of his vigilant fight against racism in the arena of civil rights. Dr. Marvin A. McMickle, one of Proctor's former associate pastors at the historic Abyssinian Baptist Church in Harlem, said on the day of his funeral: "By the thousands, there are people who feel he made the decisive impact in their lives."

Bill Moyers, award-winning journalist, gave this tribute in the year of Proctor's retirement: "Like the meal of loaves and fishes, you have nourished the multitude and lived your life as a miracle." Marian Wright Edelman, founder and CEO of the Children's Defense Fund, said, "His writings and sermons ground[ed] me with his realism and awe[d] me with his infinite optimism and faith. And he never fail[ed] to make me laugh."

I am inspired each time I recall the perduring foundation of Proctor's faith: "Believing that change is possible causes one to act in harmony with such faith. As you live it out, the unseen evidence begins to appear.... This is the substance of things hoped for. And when faith is operational, strange things happen."

Remembering Martin

Martin Luther King, Jr. abides in the annals of human history as the leader of one of the greatest liberation movements the world has ever beheld. Combining the glorious wisdom of his African-American heritage, the profound depths of his Christian convictions, and the inspiration of his powerful oratory as a Baptist preacher, King arrived at a pivotal moment in U.S. history and rose to its demands and responsibilities.

Millions have inherited the fruits of King's labors, enjoying the maturation of the U.S. Constitution and the Bill of Rights and the fuller enfranchisement of all citizens. Youthful souls have found in King a hero worthy of admiration and emulation. Generations of clergy and laity have been inspired by King's eloquence and his example of creative leadership and sacrificial service.

Among King's signal allegiances were:

- Sympathy for people from all walks of life, especially those who are poor, the left out, the left behind and the left-over.

- Loyalty to the figure of Jesus — as exemplar for social relations and as savior in one's own personal spiritual quest.

- Fidelity to the prophetic preaching tradition of the African-American pulpit, founded upon the testimony of the Hebrew prophets.

- Steadfast dissatisfaction with the status quo ("business-as-usual") — in business, politics, social policy, international affairs, and ecclesial matters.

- Openness and receptivity to the graces of new ideas, new tactics, new insights about human life and the ever-expanding possibilities for its betterment.

- Faithful practice of the principles of nonviolence.

- A belief in the power of language — inherited from the African-American religious experience — to transform individuals, communities, society, and nation-states.

King's consistent courage was a marvel to witness. While he is now nearly deified in annual commemorations on the occasion of the U.S. holiday named in his honor, King was often challenged and sometimes vilified during the living of his days. He was chosen to be the leader of the Montgomery Improvement Association at a time when most other leaders feared that nothing could ever be changed in any sector of the segregationist South. With the co-leadership of his close friend and favorite preacher Gardner C. Taylor, he helped to create a new expression of American Protestantism, the Progressive National Baptist Convention. During one of the most dramatic civil rights campaigns in Birmingham, Alabama, King drew the ire of seeming allies when he penned his "Letter from Birmingham Jail" addressing the recalcitrance and "gradualism" of his supposedly progressive fellow clergy there and elsewhere. His opposition to the Vietnam war, leading up to and including his clarifying speech "Beyond Vietnam: A Time to Break Silence: Declaration of Independence from the War in Vietnam," caused him to be roundly castigated by religious and civil rights leaders across the nation as they accused him of mixing civil rights and war.

King's theology and personal ethos were deeply rooted in his identity as an African-American Baptist preacher. Scholars have long admired King's intellect and erudition, while at the same time acknowledging that who King was and what he became were largely a result of his being a child of the African-American church. He was always appreciative of Scripture, particularly the power of the prophets and the ethics of Jesus, and he regularly counseled the traditional practices of worship, praise, and prayer for the spiritual benefit of his congregants and indeed all people.

King was a Baptist preacher in a traditional sense, always ready to proclaim the truth of God's gospel of love and justice to all hearers. Not all the venues he visited were actual sanctuaries, but whenever he spoke they became such. He was also a traditional Baptist preacher in his offering, in nearly all public occasions, an "altar call" — to social change, to personal transformation, to community redemption, to salvation. In his leadership of the American civil rights movement, his focus on the motto and mission statement of the Southern Christian

Leadership Conference was urgent and clear: "To Save the Soul of America."

One of the more prominent motifs in King's theology was his unflagging belief that "unearned suffering is redemptive." In fact, King held that the power of unearned suffering could prompt the redemption of an individual, a circumstance, and even a nation: "Somehow we must be able to stand up before our most bitter opponents and say: 'We shall match your capacity to inflict suffering by our capacity to endure suffering. We will meet your physical force with soul force. Do to us what you will and we will still love you.'"

King is rightly appreciated as one of the premier proponents of nonviolence as an effective organizing principle and tactic for social change. King was not the first nor the fiercest nonviolent activist in the United States; Howard Thurman and Mordecai Johnson had supported the strategy of Gandhian nonviolence before King was born. But it was King who crystalized the searing truth about the catastrophic danger of violence in a globe studded with countless nuclear weapons: "The choice today is no longer between violence and nonviolence; it's nonviolence or nonexistence."

King's challenges regarding economic inequities suffered by the poor at the hands of rapacious greed were made crystal clear in his most famous oration, his "I Have A Dream" speech on the steps of the Lincoln Memorial in Washington, D.C., on August 28, 1963, one hundred years after Lincoln's pronouncement of the Emancipation Proclamation: "America has given the Negro people a bad check; a check which has come back marked 'insufficient funds.'" At the end of his life, he was leading SCLC to prepare for a Poor People's Campaign event in Washington, D.C. And he was assassinated on the balcony of the Lorraine Motel in Memphis, Tennessee, the morning after he soared to heights of eloquence with his "I've Been to the Mountaintop" address before a crowd at the Mason Temple Church of God in Christ in support of striking sanitation workers. To the end of his life, King held fast to a hope for the creation of what Josiah Royce first called "the beloved community."

Gratitude for Gardner C. Taylor

When a comprehensive American religious history of the 20th century is finally compiled, the magisterial preaching eloquence of the Rev. Dr. Gardner C. Taylor will be remembered with astonishment and abiding, awe-struck admiration.

For more than 70 years, Dr. Taylor held forth among African-American Baptists and a panoramic array of religious adherents throughout the United States and around the world as an orator with few if any peers.

Only a handful of pastors know the grace of being in one pulpit for 42 years as Dr. Taylor knew it at the Concord Baptist Church of Christ in Brooklyn. Few preachers are equipped with intelligence and insight sufficient to inspire a life-long capacity for learning, as Dr. Taylor continued to experience even as a nonagenarian. Few preachers are allowed to call eminent, historically significant personages "close friends," as Dr. Taylor easily did with Martin Luther King, Jr.

Described by magazines as the "Dean of Black Preaching" and the "poet laureate of American Protestantism," Dr. Taylor was deemed "one of the 12 most effective preachers in the English-speaking world" in a 1996 Baylor University survey.

Foremost in the treasury of Dr. Taylor's gifts was his felicity with language. Steeped in the blessings of the African-American Christian heritage, the son of an eloquent preacher father and a devout teacher mother, Dr. Taylor also knew the deep riches in the history of Christian proclamation. He was on close personal terms with the language and thought of the great British and Scottish preachers of previous centuries, the plentiful traditions of the Church universal, as well as the long trajectory of faithful proclamation witnessed in the Bible.

MLK's Favorite Preacher

As pastor of the Concord Baptist Church and afterwards in retirement, Dr. Taylor engaged the issues of his community, the nation, and the world with passion, insight, and effectiveness. He artfully combined the necessary durative dynamic of transcendence with the equally necessary punctiliar character of incarnation.

With Martin Luther King, Jr., who called Dr. Taylor his "favorite" preacher, he helped found the Progressive National Baptist Convention in order for congregations to better address and overcome the ravages of racism and segregation in the United States. Working from the North, he led the Concord church and many other congregations to raise funds for Dr. King's efforts in the South.

Dr. Taylor also served on the New York City Board of Education and was always involved in issues that arose in the "public square" of Brooklyn and greater New York. In his later years, Dr. Taylor worried that many religious leaders and their congregations had lost their "prophetic edge" and might fall into the trap of merely mirroring a "consumeristic culture."

Compassion Sabbath in Kansas City

Whenever he spoke and wherever he travelled, Dr. Taylor dealt with ethical issues and matters of public significance, including when he came to Kansas City.

The Center for Practical Bioethics will remain abidingly thankful for Dr. Taylor's presence in Kansas City in 1999 at the launching of "Compassion Sabbath," which engaged more than 80,000 faith-community leaders and members in hundreds of congregations in an interfaith initiative to increase the quality of care for those facing the end of life. At a breakfast gathering at Union Station, he spoke compellingly of the need for honesty and compassion in relation to the experience of debilitation and pain at the end of life.

During the time of a sabbatical journey in 2010, I was privileged to share a long conversation with Dr. Taylor in his home in Raleigh, North Carolina. In retirement, Dr. Taylor echoed in his meditations what he put forth as a preacher, pastor, and activist for the betterment of humanity. He spoke plainly and with swift clarity about the process of aging. When what he prayed for, he said his personal prayers were "to get out without too much pain." And he added, with a chuckle, "And I'm ready to get out, I'm ready to go."

People in the pew, the academy of homileticians, and awestruck fellow clergy regarded Dr. Taylor as a singular personality whose like only comes around once every century or so. We would agree and only add that we're so glad that he came to Kansas City to share his extraordinary voice for the intertwining for what is "good" and what is "right."

(This is a significantly augmented version of a piece I wrote for the Center for Practical Bioethics' blog, just shortly after Dr. Taylor passed away on Easter Sunday, April 5, 2015.)

Osip Mandelstam, Modern Psalmist

For being alive, for the joy of calm breath, / tell me, who should I bless?

Normally we would expect to find lines like these in the book of Psalms. When we discover such poetry in a modern context, our attention is arrested. I came across them when I responded to the suggestion of a friend and searched for the work of Osip Mandelstam.

Now, admittedly, Mandelstam is hardly a household name in the United States, or in Russia where he lived and died, or in Poland, the land of his birth. And yet his poetry and poetic influence live on with grace and power.

In Mandelstam's own time during the first portion of the 20th century, he would come to be admired in a circle of great artists of his generation, including his friend Anna Akhmatova.

Like the Psalter, Mandelstam's words stir the imagination, quicken the impulse of gratitude, and ennoble the soul. His good, solid words convey a love for the world God has given, even when one is in distress.

One of my favorite Mandelstam poems contains the following phrase: "I love this poor earth, / for I have not yet known another."

For the joys of reading lines such as these, which are eloquent echoes of the sentiments of the Psalms, I know Whom to bless.

Mordecai Wyatt Johnson: Strategic, Visionary Hopefulness

As we enter Black History Month, a flood of images and icons rushes to center stage: the determination of Rosa Parks, the unvanquished spirit of Sojourner Truth, the courageous fidelity of Harriet Tubman, the stirring righteousness of Frederick Douglass, the tenacity of Ida B. Wells, the magisterial presence of Paul Robeson, the sacred audacity of Fannie Lou Hamer, the scientific mastery of George Washington Carver, the legendary revivalistic preaching of Caesar A.W. Clark, the searing prescience of W.E.B. Du Bois, the lyricism of Maya Angelou, the theological genius of Howard Thurman, and, of course, the eloquent rhetoric and life of Martin Luther King. This year I'm also remembering another figure less well known but no less significant than all the other celebrated exemplars.

In 1926, Mordecai Wyatt Johnson became the first African-American president of Howard University. Johnson would go on to invite Dr. Thurman and his wife Sue Bailey Thurman to join the faculty and then, nearly a decade later, to encourage them to go on a Pilgrimage of Friendship to India where they would be among the first four African-Americans to meet and have deep discussions with Mohandas K. Gandhi. Thurman would then bear the tenets of nonviolence to the United States, where he would convey the Mahatma's insights to generations of adherents who would lead the civil rights struggle toward its fulfillment.

When he began, however, Mordecai Wyatt Johnson had another primary concern: raising the standards of Howard's law school, which was then little more than a night school. Supreme Court Associate Justice Louis D. Brandeis counseled Johnson, emphasizing that the foundation for overcoming racial discrimination was embedded in the Constitution. "What was needed," Brandeis averred, "was for lawyers to be prepared to base their arguments before the Court precisely upon the guarantees in the document."

Agreeing with Brandeis' thesis and taking his counsel to heart, Mordecai Johnson secured Charles Hamilton Houston as vice-dean of the Howard University School of Law in 1929, and things got moving. An initial class of students was eventually enrolled in Howard University's now accredited, full-time program with an intensified civil rights curriculum.

Johnson and Houston were bound and determined to train top-notch, world-class lawyers who would lead the fight against racial injustice. Among the seven graduates of Howard's Law School in 1930 was a young man named Thurgood Marshall.

The rest, as they say, is history. Marshall would go on to lead the successful Brown v. Board of Education case that abolished legal segregation in public education in the United States. Eventually he became the first African-American appointed to the Supreme Court.

Mordecai Wyatt Johnson and Charles Hamilton Houston were not the only ones to lead America toward the dismantling of institutional prejudice in the 20th century, but their unflagging strategic, visionary hopefulness contributed mightily to the transformation of American culture and the promise of American democracy for one and all.

Strategic, visionary hopefulness. This is what is required to make for greater "Racial Justice" for one and all.

In Appreciation of "God's Will"

Will Campbell was one of the most powerful witnesses for the Christian faith that the United States ever beheld. Born a son of the deep South, baptized in a Mississippi creek, educated at a Connecticut seminary, seasoned in the U.S. Army, matured in a university chaplaincy, Will eventually became perhaps the most important white man in the modern civil rights movement.

During tumultuous times in the South, he served as "a field staff member" for the National Council of Churches. He was with Dr. Martin Luther King, Jr., at the founding of the Southern Christian Leadership Conference. He ministered at the now-hallowed locales of the great civil rights hallmarks — Selma and Little Rock and Montgomery and Washington, D.C. — at those times when the heart of our nation and the souls of its citizens were transformed irrevocably.

I'm one of many who always treasured Will's counsel and friendship, which commenced for me when I was making my way through seminary in Nashville and afterwards working with prisoners, ex-prisoners, and their families in an organization called "Project Return." In addition to his work in civil rights, Will also helped establish a coalition of prison ministries — the largest of its kind at that time — across the South.

At his comfortable home nestled on a small farm in Mt. Juliet, Tennessee, Will was a source of friendly conversation, scriptural commentary, prayerful support, and loads of wisdom-soaked, hilarity-tinted stories, for me and for countless others who shared a common bond of admiration and affection for their "Brother Will."

For all of us Will was a "sacred sibling," the kind of uncle you may not see very often but can always depend on for compassion and wisdom.

Fortunately, there are a goodly number of books and films about and by Will. To learn about this singular character whose life and legacy teaches more about justice and mercy than we could ever hope collectively to master, check out his best novel, *The Glad River*. Or you may be intrigued by his children's book, *Chester and Chun Ling*. Or you may be inspired by the Alabama Arts Council's *Brother Will* video which was produced for public television in 2012. Or, perhaps, best of all, you will search for a 25th anniversary copy of Will's award-winning autobiography *Brother to a Dragonfly,* which now includes a forward by President Jimmy Carter.

In encounters with these and many other tomes, one cannot help but grow into a deep appreciation for what Will meant for the Church in all of its manifestations in the U.S. and what he meant for justice and grace in the civil rights movement.

In the end, God's will worked itself out in extraordinary fashion in "God's Will." As we remember Will, let us say "Thanks be to God" and continue to work for dignity and grace to be accorded to all of God's children.

George Tiller's Tragic Death

The murder of Dr. George Tiller, on Pentecost Sunday, May 31, 2009, at his home church in Wichita, Kansas, is a heinous act that should sadden all hearts. This latest violence exacerbates the divisive debates that have attended the issue of abortion for nearly two generations, debates that have left Americans heartbroken and soul-weary.

It's obvious there isn't sufficient time or circumstance here to disentangle the competing claims regarding scientific, medical, ethical and/or spiritual "facts" which various camps believe about human life's beginnings. Still, all people of faith should be on guard against self-righteousness, something which Jesus and the Hebrew prophets before him consistently and adamantly warned against. And everyone needs to avoid any inclination to demonize (and thus dehumanize) those with whom they disagree.

Regarding the gamut of reproduction issues, I have no quarrel with various religious groups taking stances against abortion, birth control, fertility regimens, or *in vitro* fertilization, and then enacting guidelines for themselves.

But I'm profoundly glad that birth control is now universally available for U.S. citizens who want it, that *in vitro* fertilization and fertility regimens are legal and safe options for previously infertile couples, and that safe and legal abortions are provided for rape and incest victims. And I will remain vigilant in advocating to maintain the legality of those procedures and options while at the same time working diligently to prevent unwelcome pregnancies.

What is paramount for Americans at this time, I believe, is a "dialing down" of what can, at best, be called a "rhetoric of vehemence," a way of pressing one's opinions that exudes from a fanatical and exclusionary fundamentalism. Acts of violence like the senseless slaying of George Tiller in church this past Sunday, and others before him, are too often the result of such vitriolic speech and reckless political beliefs.

We are presently called to pray for the solace of Dr. Tiller's family and for the soul of the perpetrator, as well. Let justice now prevail, and let us proceed with calmer minds, softer edges, more tender hearts, and a more finely tuned grasp of the complications and nuanced situations involved in difficult ethical issues.

Remembering Pat McGeachy

Remembering the Rev. Dr. Daniel Patrick McGeachy III (November 19, 1929 – December 13, 2015)

  The death of Pat McGeachy leaves a God-shaped hole in life — in the lives of those who loved and admired him and of those whom he loved and cared for, and in my life.
  I came to know Pat through Project Return, an agency he helped to found and which was housed for several years at Downtown Presbyterian Church in Nashville, Tennessee. In May of 1980, two days after receiving my M.Div. from Vanderbilt Divinity School, I went to work at Project Return with Kit Kuperstock. Others would join in Project Return's work, focusing on assisting people leaving prisons and jails with a solid sense of welcome in the free world, job placement assistance, and some not infrequent kick-in-the-tail counseling. Because some of the staff were also ministers, there were also occasional invitations to preside at weddings and funerals.
  The atmosphere in Project Return's office, right down the hall from Pat's office, was, as Pat once described it, like unto the story line and subjects of the television show "M.A.S.H.": complicated, comical, and always dealing with life situations that portended wonder-filled fortune and/or damnable tragedy. Kit and I, along with co-workers Rudy Chatman, Nolan Eagan, Michael Bailey, Harmon Wray, Robert Arnold, Bill Frith, Stuart Kuperstock, Tara Seeley, Michele Munson, Betsy Pankey, Kathleen Danforth, and a slew of field placement folks and interns from Vandy and volunteers from other non-profit groups around Nashville, worked together for good purpose and always with a healthy dose of humbling hilarity.
  It was through Project Return and through DPC's weekly lunch program that I was privileged to witness Pat's profligate talents as a preacher, pastor, counselor, and community leader. I had heard that he was a powerful preacher, previously at Westminster Presbyterian Church and other congregations along his intriguing career path. But I had never heard him preach until I began attending the Wednesday noon services. That service regularly offered some of the most inspiring proclamations one could hear in Nashville, or anywhere else.

Of course, Pat was a bona fide logophile, always reading and quoting every notable writer and source to anyone who would listen. He was an excellent writer himself, too. While I was at Project Return, I was graced to read and then be gifted with a copy of his doctoral dissertation, a commentary on the 13th chapter of Paul's first epistle to the cantankerous group of early Christians at the church at Corinth. I still have it and take counsel from Pat's words whenever I'm preaching or teaching on Paul's great "love hymn."

Pat was a genuine reveler. He loved life and wanted everyone else to love it too. He took extreme delight in music, not only with his guitar, which he used to great effect in church settings and at some of the parties he and Alice hosted, but in all of its multitudinous expressions.

But Pat's revelry wasn't limited to music. He could also tell a good joke (and more than a few horribly pun-infused ones), and he could play some unparalleled practical jokes on friends. Once he called me on my extension at Project Return, exclaiming, "Hey, Hill, there's a dead woman in my office!" I slammed down the phone and raced down the church hallway into his office, blurting out, "What happened? Who do we need to call? Shouldn't we call an ambulance or the police or someone??" But there was no body to be seen or found anywhere. "What's going on, Pat?" I asked. He pointed to a box wrapped in brown paper on a bookshelf and said, "There she is." It was the cremains of a church member who had requested that he kindly dispose of her ashes at an appropriate time and place, and the box had just arrived via special delivery.

Pat proffered enormous gifts as a friend, tenderly offering free cedar trees at Christmas, hospitality to folks at holiday times, laugh-saturated lunches, book recommendations, eloquent recollections of movies and plays, and unrelenting regalings about the wondrous ways of his children and his beloved Alice.

Pat's passion for justice was persistently strong and unfailing, an attribute I much admired and saw as a pastoral trait to emulate. He advocated persuasively and enduringly for others, and the perduring presence of Project Return and other social ministry programs is a significant part of his legacy.

But his ministry and his life, I believe, were always and ultimately seasoned with mercy. Nearly every December, I go back in my mind's eye to the steps outside the Project Return doors on the southeast corner of the Downtown Presbyterian Church edifice. It was there that a group of three adults with Down syndrome were stranded in the midst of a horrific snowstorm. The transportation that was scheduled to carry them home from their sheltered workshop activity had been clogged up somewhere, and they were shivering in the cold waiting for some unknown bus that was likewise frozen in the impossible traffic situation that had descended on Nashville that late December afternoon. We ushered them into Project Return's office and got them coffee and hot chocolate and secured the needed information about where they lived. Then Pat and I directed them to his SUV (an International Harvester Scout, as I recall), and off we went to deliver them home, a feat made possible by some adventurous driving on Pat's part. It was Matthew 25 and Micah 6:8 and the essence of the Christmas story all rolled into one memorable event.

While his devotion to family was exemplary and his interpretation of scripture was consistently profound (and unusual) and his gifts with music were impressive (and unique) and his original limericks were unparalleled in my experience (and creatively earthy, to boot), it was Pat's enthusiasm for life itself and the extraordinary dimensions of everyday sacredness that I'll most remember. That, and his ability to sum up broad concepts in brief statements and formulas.

I will always associate the word "Joy" with Pat. I remember Pat once describing "J.O.Y." as consisting of three ways of loving:

1. Loving Jehovah (God).
2. Loving Others (Neighbor).
3. Loving Yourself (Self).

At the time of my ordination I was blessed mightily when a special chasuble Pat had made was placed over my head after the laying on of hands. On the front side of the chasuble were the initials "J.O.Y.," signaling his memorable definition and his hope and wish for the ministry upon which I was embarking. Now, 35 years after that moment and Pat's generosity, I still believe that being joyful in those three ways is the hallmark of what it means to be a faithful pastor, preacher, leader, and friend. "J.O.Y." was certainly writ large and legible in Pat and the life he shared with others. Having been graced by Pat and his "J.O.Y.," I can't imagine a better way to live.

Blaisdell Blessedness

Whenever Christmas comes around, I go to the Blaisdells. Maybe not literally, but figuratively and imaginatively and spiritually, at least. Their home became a welcoming haven, and ultimately my home, at crucial stages of my life, and most especially at Christmas.

I recall spending several Christmases in the warmth of their home in Ft. Worth, Texas, during the halcyon days of college. And I can remember like it was yesterday, one holiday time during my graduate school tenure: driving in the dead of night from Nashville, Tennessee to Ft. Worth, through wretched weather, enduring one of the wheels literally falling off of my car, just so I could be in the Blaisdell's living room on Christmas morning.

Chuck Blaisdell was and remains one of my dearest friends. We've known each other since the topsy-turvy days of high school Christian Youth Fellowship conferences. When I arrived at Texas Christian University in Ft. Worth, it was through Chuck that I met his parents Hazel and Dick and that their home became a joyful dwelling place for me.

Sunday afternoons at the Blaisdells meant the Dallas Cowboys and brisket. Thanksgiving meant turkey (and at least a week's worth of turkey soup) and games of Risk and Monopoly until the wee hours. And Christmas meant grace and comfort and cherry tarts. (To this day, cherry tarts are a necessary portion of our home's Christmas morning rituals.) And the blustery days of Super Bowl weekend meant chili and a persistent debate about which Cowboys team was the greatest of all time.

In time Chuck's brothers Jim and Greg would also become beloved to me. Despite time and distance, I cannot imagine anything I would not do for them if they asked me. (Jacob and Esau grew apart over time, too. But as a sign of my esteem for Chuck's brothers I would echo Jacob's sentiment when he embraced Esau in reunion at long last: "truly to see your face is like seeing the face of God, with such favor have you received me.")

It was Hazel and Dick, however, who provided the strong, mysterious, and lasting attachment to Christmas for me. Among all the wonderful people whose hospitality I have been privileged to enjoy, the Blaisdells remain the ultimate expression of what Christmas is all about: a treasuring of simple, lastingly good relationships, good events, good food; mercy; and jubilation at the daily gifts life brings one and all. Their loving warmth was unconditional. Their affectionate affirmation was abiding and gracious. Their joyous gratitude was deep and profound, their hospitality irrefutably genuine.

To put it simply, the Blaisdells made a place for me in the hearts and their home, and because of their tender mercies, I was born anew. What I received from the Blaisdells I suppose I would call "Blaisdell blessedness" — as beautiful as new-fallen snow, as exquisite as a baby's smile, as essential for a fully developed life as the air we all breathe.

Every year the same item is inscribed at the top of my Christmas wish list: that everyone — family and friends and acquaintances and strangers — may experience good portions of "Blaisdell blessedness" during the high holiday times. It is one of the best ways I know of to get close to a certain manger in Bethlehem.

Encomium for Michael Zedek

May 1, 2016

Dear Michael,

Besides what I said at *your* "first retirement," allow me this moment to convey to you my heartfelt thanks for your generous affirmations and celebrations last June at *my* "first retirement." You were and are, as you always have been, caring and kind.

Allow me, also, on the occasion of your "second retirement," to observe that "This is it!" If you or I ever have another retirement, let us celebrate with merely a nod or a whisper, or, maybe, a cyberspace citation.

For who are you kidding? Retiring? Really? Here I recall Jimmy Dugan, manager for the Rockford Peaches in the movie *A League of Their Own,* declaring his incredulity in the face of anguishing sorrow expressed by one of his female charges: "Crying? There's no crying in baseball!"

And so, in parallel fashion, "Retiring? There's no retiring for Rabbi Michael Zedek!"

So what is the occasion of your retirement from the position of senior rabbi of Emanuel Congregation in Chicago, Illinois, on May 1, 2016, really for? Allow me to hazard an alternative to *retirement.* In addition to celebrating the sterling fulfillment of your role as senior rabbi at Emanuel Congregation, I think the reason a mighty throng of your congregants and friends gather together is to herald your *transformation* from settled rabbi to roving rabbi, fierce rebel full of finesse, and raconteur extraordinaire.

In other words, you are putting your show on the road, a show resplendent with intelligence, wit, and always — always! — deep compassion for those under the shelter of your shepherding — indeed, for all humanity. Emanuel Congregation is now commissioning you into a larger realm, a broader reach, a wider embrace.

As you enter into your newest transformation, I'm reminded of Herman Wouk, the great novelist and the first recipient of the Library of Congress Lifetime Achievement Award. I'm reminded of Herman Wouk at this time not because of his blockbuster *Winds of War* and *War and Remembrance,* nor because of his engrossing take on his bone-deep experience of Judaism in *This Is My God*. I'm reminded of Herman Wouk on the occasion your retirement because of his most recent book, *Sailor and Fiddler: Reflections of a 100-Year-Old Author*, and what he says there about the twinned blessings of "literature" and "writing for a living." What's at stake in literature, Wouk says, is "one's heart's blood." Alternately, he avers, "writing for a living is something else entirely."

Michael, being a rabbi is what you have done for a living. That is, after all, what a contract between a congregation and a rabbi is for, I suppose. You have made a living (and a life) as a rabbi. And your output has been prodigious and powerful at Emanuel. But in the process of being a rabbi making a living, you have also contributed mightily to "literature," so to speak, a "literature" of love and grace, a "literature" wrought from a sacred source, your own "heart's blood."

For both your own rabbinical "writing for a living" and contributing to the sacred "literature" of your own "heart's blood" which you have shared so abundantly and generously with others, I join a horde your friends, colleagues, and congregants, and say "Thanks!"

As I convey my "Thanks!" I also want to say "Go!" But on the occasion of your retirement (but never retiring), at this juncture of yet another of your transformations, perhaps "Go" is too pedestrian of a word.

Perhaps another word, a synonym, for "Go" would be better. Well, I've got one for you, arising from the verbiage of cosmic silliness that was part of the most fantastically successfully sitcoms in the history of television. While its concluding episode left a lot to be desired, the treasured characters were all there, as they had been in the previous seasons and as they would be in syndication: Elaine, beautiful and flighty and irascible. Nefarious Newman, the portly postman. George Costanza, the most pathetic partner ever created for any TV buddy. And, of course, Jerry himself, the ultimate "non-buddy" buddy, whose name in real-life gave the fictional show its title, *Seinfeld*.

But there was one more character in that show, an unrepeatable character, after whom they definitely broke the mold: Cosmo Kramer. And it is from Kramer that we are bequeathed a synonym for "Go."

Whenever Kramer was jubilant, whenever he was recruiting his friends to join him in a worthy pursuit, whenever he was excited about the prospects of something new and grand about to happen, he would exclaim "Giddyup!"

And that's what I commend to you now, dear friend, as you embark on this latest of your adventures into a fulfilling life: Go! Giddyup!

Giddyup! Go into the future with continuing vitality and vibrancy, for the whole world desperately needs your special brand of those qualities.

Giddyup! Continue to go to every person who has ever given up on faith being an experience that can be called both relevant and "revelant." You have a nearly indefatigable capacity as a witness for the timeliness, the timelessness, and the searing truths of Judaism.

Giddyup! Go to the least, the left behind, and the left out and continue to assure them that they can make it. Given the ever-widening gulf between the rich and the poor, your voice is needed now more than ever before.

Giddyup! Go to the young and the not-so-young, anyone and everyone who is cynical, jaded, skeptical about anything ever changing, go to those who have capitulated to "the way things always are," and share your extraordinary vision of possibilities yet undreamt and powers yet untapped.

Go. Giddyup. Godspeed and abundant blessings in your going!

Love,
Bob

Margaret Smith — Celebration of Life

January 30, 2016 – Vantage House, Columbia, Maryland

I

Good morning. My name is Bob Hill, and in what I say in a minute, you will note how I can only refer to Lex and Margaret Smith —as I and all of their nieces and nephews have always affectionately called them— as Uncle Doc and Aunt Margaret.

On behalf of my sisters and myself, I want to say, again, Uncle Doc, that our mother, Bennie Lee Smith Hill, made a great decision to designate you as legal guardian for Mary Beth and Becky. And while it was surely excruciating for them to live beyond our mother's too early death, you and Aunt Margaret provided stability and reassurance in a difficult time. You and Aunt Margaret stood in the gap, and it's hard to imagine what would have transpired if you had not been there as Becky and Mary Beth proceeded through high school toward college.

II

I always recollect Aunt Margaret as "the queen of spring cleaning." I can't ever recall our mother being so fastidious and thorough. I also can't remember anyone who used mothballs as thoroughly as Aunt Margaret did. In fact, the first time I ever smelled that distinctive aroma was while visiting at 5904 Meadowood Rd., during summer vacation. My associations with your home on Meadowood Road are seared into my memory, and I can recall 5904 Meadowood Rd., Baltimore, Maryland, 21212, as clearly as I can my home address in Brownsville, Texas, 3465 Hipp Ave. And that pungent mothball smell is clearly in my memory now.

III

But, beyond the spring cleaning, I can also recall Aunt Margaret's wonderful German potato salad. Tasting that dish was unique in my experience as a child. I knew the cold sort of potato salad, sweet, with pickle relish, but had never savored the warm, tangy taste of German potato salad until Aunt Margaret introduced it to me.

IV

I'll always remember Aunt Margaret for her straightforwardness. While her origins were in Alpine, Texas, she didn't dwell in the alpine region of abstraction. Rather, in all of her intelligence and inquisitiveness about life, she showed forth a preference for the concrete, the real, the practical. That was her focus. And what a needful posture that is. Others may dwell with their heads in the clouds — the imaginative is, of course, essential to our humanness. But the ones with their feet on the ground are the ones who get done what needs to be done.

V

"Interesting" is another way that I'll remember Aunt Margaret. Oh, I don't mean the dismissive way some people use the word "interesting," say, when a group of friends is trying to figure out which movie to go to, and you suggest one, and one of the group says, "Oh, hmmm, that would be interesting." No, rather, Aunt Margaret found others and their lives interesting. Whenever I was around her I felt that she was intrigued by the lives of others and found their lives truly interesting. Her interest was an expression of her sincere caring for you, her concern for your welfare and well-being.

VI

Psalm 46 relates to our situation in the wake of Aunt Margaret's death. "There is a river," Psalm 46 declares, "that shall make glad the city of [the divine.] God is in the midst of her. She shall not be moved." The city is obviously the idealized Jerusalem, or it could be the much-longed-for, ultimate city of realized reconciliation and fulfilled hope. Such a city points to a future time when "all shall be well, and all manner of things shall be well," as one mystic put it. And that's a helpful reminder today, with much healing in its wings. For despite whatever heartache and sense of loss we may experience in the wake of Aunt Margaret's death, there is hope, and no little consolation, in memory. In the collective remembrance of Aunt Margaret, especially in the lives of Jim, and Mary B, and Barbara, and all of your children, and your children's children — all those who, we may say, wear her genes — the good prevails and the untoward fades and love abides. If my faith is about anything, it is about this: "the worst things are never the last things."

As one philosopher put it at the passing of one of his beloveds, "And in the night of death, hope sees a star, and listening love hears the rustle of a wing."

Which is what another psalm, Psalm 42, also declares when it proclaims that "deep calls to deep at the thunder of thy cataracts," before which we stand in awe-filled wonder.

Which is what we are doing. Deep is calling unto deep. The depths of Aunt Margaret's life — and all that she did and felt and all those whom she cared for and loved — are calling to the depths of your life and my life. And as deep calls unto deep, we are awash in wonder and filled with grace. And such experiences, such wonders, such graces are sheer gifts beyond any rational reckoning.

VII

May we leave from this place remembering Aunt Margaret with the words of Dag Hammarskjöld, the U.N. Secretary-General whose posthumously published book *Markings* was an inspiration to Aunt Margaret's generation: "For all that has been — Thanks! To all that shall be — Yes!"

WHAT IT MEANS TO BE A MINISTER

All You Need Is More Love

A Call to Ministry

The call to the ordained ministry came for me:
1. Quickly, like a shout,
2. Then consistently, like a long strong pull,
3. And then, after much prayer and reflection, as a resolute decision.

From an early age, my involvement in the church was enriching and enlivening. Almost always, I loved being "at church" and pondering what I had learned from Sunday School teachers and in worship services.

Once, during a dream as a seven-year-old, while comparing the creation stories I had learned in Sunday School with an astronomy lesson about infinite space I had learned at public school, I woke with a startled shout at the sheer magnificence of God's power over all the world: "Wow, God is big!" I suppose that something of God's call was in that disruptive dream.

Then came the long strong pull. It was at church that I learned that healthy differences of opinions were not only allowable, but sure signs of a healthy community. It was at church that my parent's divorce was soothed by a comforting embrace of understanding and sensitivity. It was at church that the shock of my mother's death (when all three of her children including myself, then a high school senior, had not left our teenage years) was annealed and healed by warm fellowship and care.

Early on, too — in reference to leadership activities in the local church youth group and other capacities associated with the Gulf Coast area of the Christian Church (Disciples of Christ) — it seemed to me that people said, "He can talk good." Before too long I began considering the notion that there might be a place for me in the leadership of the church that would entail speaking and teaching and other public presentations.

But the call, however quickly it seemed to come in that shouting moment of early childhood years, or the long strong pull of teenage years, was muted, for a while, by the seeming irrelevance of the church during the 1960s and early 1970s.

At All Peoples Christian Church and Community Center in Los Angeles, California — to which I travelled in 1972 and where I served until 1974 to fulfill my conscientious objector's alternative service obligation — the call became a momentous occasion for decision.

At All Peoples, the Church was so obviously:

- relevant and real,
- charming and challenging,
- service-oriented and celebratory,
- justice-related and jubilant,
- kind and keen,
- tough and tender,
- loving and level-headed,
- gritty and glory-bound.

After my time at All Peoples my educational direction was clear, my vocational destiny was resolved, and the earlier callings were now a confirmed clarion call to the ordained ministry.

Reflections on Being a Pastor ... Here, Now, and With Joy!

From time to time, it is good to remind ourselves of the conditions that make for a pastor's best work.

HERE: When you think about it, where else can you be but *here*, or the *here* wherever you are? *Being here* is more than mere proximity but rather the quality of attentiveness.

Being *here* with others — being present and accounted for — is one of the premier gifts which pastors offer to others — in worship, at the wedding altar, at the hospital bedside, around a table, at the graveside, in a home, or even over the phone or via email — in times of celebration and times of sorrow.

NOW: Respect for tradition and enthusiasm for the future are twin chambers of the same faithful heart. We cannot have one without the other.

"New occasions teach new duties," rightly proclaims one insightful hymn. And yet both our honored yesterdays and anticipated tomorrows are known best by the lens of today. Without the transforming power of a present focus, we abide either in nostalgia or fantasy.

Only now, today — which, by the way, was one of Jesus' favorite words — is faith best realized.

JOY: From the gleeful face of a newly baptized child to the warm glow of seven-dozen birthday candles reflected in an 84-year-old's eyes, from the delight generated by gifts of food and water in a time of drought to the happiness in clergy and congregation alike when a word is fitly spoken, from the cradle to the crypt, we are challenged to "count it all joy."

The principle remains true: the more joy pastors receive, convey, and help create for and with others, the more joy will prevail in congregations, and the more joy will gladden the heart of God.

Spiritual Checkup

Have you had your annual "spiritual checkup"? We regularly make appointments — or at least we're *supposed* to make such appointments — with our physician and other relevant medical personnel regarding our physical health.

We are bombarded daily with media messages about healthier lifestyles, healthier foods, healthier exercises, healthier workout equipment, and the eternal quest for healthier-looking bodies.

Yet in a culture clamoring about health, we rarely speak cogently of the various aspects of our spiritual health. Let us resolve that now is the time for a refocusing of our time, energy, and resources on those qualities, verities, and values which matter in the ultimate dimensions of our lives. Let us resolve to have good *diets*, engage in disciplined *exercise*, and maintain an altogether healthy spiritual *lifestyle*. And as we resolve so to do, let us consider the following ingredients which may stand as a *prescription* for our spiritual health.

1. **Worship**: The experience of regular worship — which includes times of praise, celebration, reflection, and renewal — definitely magnifies our spiritual health. Worship is both an exercise that keeps our spiritual muscles of praise and celebration nimble and supple, and a necessary "minimum nutrition requirement" in our existential diet.

2. **Fellowship**: Experiences which bring us into contact with others on a similar quest always make us spiritually healthier. Fellowship is both the practice which conditions the church "team" for its performance in the "game of life," and a time for refreshing rest and relaxation. Fellowship may be the most neglected and yet most needed component in the lives of some who are seeking spiritual health.

3. **Study**: Study is both exercise and diet when it comes to the spiritual health of a Christian. Regularly using a devotional book, opening one's Bible and subsequently one's mind and heart to the truths therein, shared discussion about life choices, passionate engagement

pertaining to ethical issues, cherished remembrances of the treasured stories of our sacred heritage — all of these are what keep the arteries of Christ's Body unclogged. All of these serve to lower the cholesterol of confusion and raise the aerobic metabolism of meaning for the Church.

4. **Witness and Service:** When we have worshiped well, when we have shared fellowship in faith, and when we have studied and reflected with thoroughness, then we are probably in good shape, spiritually speaking. Then we are equipped for a healthy expression of our humanity, and the holy shaping of the world. Service which witnesses to our faith in God through Christ always has a doubling-back effect: it is made possible because of proper, healthy preparation, and it makes possible yet more service, because it increases our spiritual strength.

In so many telling ways, the Church that follows the "Great Physician" Jesus is intended to be a "spiritual health organization."

God Loves the "Hilarious Giver"

"God loves the 'hilarious' giver!" This is a more literal translation of the Apostle Paul's phrase familiarly rendered as "God loves a cheerful giver." The latter version bears with it the usual connotations of giving from a posture of glad generosity. This is surely the best perspective from which to offer our gifts — time, talent and treasure — for God's ultimate purposes. However, a fresh interpretation of what "hilarious giving" means can enliven our sense of stewardship and challenge us to new heights of enlightenment.

"Hilarious giving" is motivated out of joy as well as responsibility. "Hilarious givers" share what they have with a spirit of contagious enthusiasm. "Hilarious givers" possess a great need to spread around God's good news they have received and for others to embrace God's grace with belly-laughs, and shining eyes, and nearly blinding smiles.

"Hilarious giving" is the most generous sort of giving. It wells up over a lifetime of steadfast practice and discipline. Sometimes "hilarious giving" even results in a bequest or gift after earthly life has passed, and in this way the gift keeps on giving into the future.

"Hilarious giving" can be heard in the Sunday School child's gleeful sharing of a cup of orange juice with her neighbor. "Hilarious giving" can be witnessed in an adult Sunday School teacher imparting a brand-new insight into Biblical material.

"Hilarious giving" happens whenever teenagers from the youth group participate in a service project or bake cookies to help the homeless. "Hilarious giving" occurs when a church caregiver presents the bread and the cup and a heartfelt smile to a homebound member during a moment of sacred communion.

"Hilarious giving" can be heard over the burgeoning and burdened tables of a church's bazaar. With cackles of laughter, wide-eyed wonder, and pleased countenances, volunteers give untold hours to make the bazaar a truly hilarious success. "Hilarious giving" is fun and enjoyable, granting delight and happiness to those who enact it.

"Hilarious giving" seems at times quite far from being reasonable, and that's because it is. "Hilarious giving" stands beyond pure rationality. It lies above that which is only concerned with efficiency.

"Hilarious giving," guileless and new and redemptive, wells up from deep within a believer's heart, and is transferred to others without calculation. "Hilarious giving" is the ultimate expression of faithful joy.

Stewardship

In the repository of the Christian vocabulary, one of the most important and treasured terms is the word "stewardship." It is so much more than merely a word which a congregation trots out for inspection every year during the annual campaign to elevate the resources to undergird a programming budget.

From the beginning of the Bible's striking account of humanity's course through history, stewardship is a key practical issue.

The Garden of Eden account is primarily about the appropriate stewardship of creation's wonders.

The story of Noah and the ark focusses on humanity's neglect of a proper stewardship, and a restorative fresh start for a right-minded stewardship of creaturely life on earth.

Among Jesus' many concerns, stewardship was always a very high priority.

Even the apostle Paul got in his own view of stewardship when he declared that Christians are "stewards of the mysteries of God" (I Corinthians 4:1).

A strong, steadfast, faith-filled, trusting, and loving attitude toward Christian stewardship is an amazing and empowering thing.

Generous stewardship is the elderly person living on fixed income who also fixes their pledge at a higher level each year so that a burgeoning group of young parents can bequeath a vibrant faith to their young children.

Caring stewardship is everyone doing something so that just a few don't have to do everything.

Loyal stewardship is the college-aged person who has little money to provide for God's work in the Church but who does have time and attention to offer to a church member at a nursing home.

Faithful stewardship is the man who plans for a congregation's well-being far into the future, as he makes arrangements for a planned bequest in his will.

Joyful stewardship is the whimsical soul who gives an extra-special outreach gift at a special offering, so that others might enjoy their holidays with more gladness and satisfaction.

Hopeful stewardship is the wealthy person who gives more each and every year because of the sheer satisfaction they receive from sharing their blessings.

Fledgling stewardship is a young boy and a young girl struggling to see who can be the first to put their quarters in the Heifer Project "tube" each Sunday morning as they approach the chancel for the Children's Sermon.

For all of us, may stewardship be all that and yet so much more, as Sunday comes and beyond.

The Gifts of Membership

"Membership has its privileges."

Such was the bygone advertising slogan of American Express. And it caught on so strongly in American culture because it seemed so true.

In congregations, however, there are not so much privileges as there are immense gifts.

Consider these gifts:

- Renewal (for your soul through relationships with others who seek after God's grace)
- Loving Hospitality (which you not only receive but have the double joy of offering to others in the spirit of Christ)
- Encouragement (from a loving community)
- Engagement (with issues and about things that matter the most)
- Restful Respite (from the harried-ness and busy-ness of the world)
- Welcome (in a "safe place," proffered by people who care)
- Friendships (at any time in your life, at any stage of your life)
- Belonging (without question or qualification)
- Companionship (through meaningful moments along your journey)
- Beauty (in art, in worship, in the faces of your cohorts in faith)
- Empowerment (for the living of your days with purpose and joy)
- Grace (tendered regularly and generously from God through the hands and hearts of sojourners and seekers like you)

Surely there are umpteen other gifts you could also list. Consider them all as you make your way to worship this weekend and offer a prayer of thanks for each one.

Weddings

Among the sacred rites that touch a community of faith, none is so full of surprising joys and so fraught with unexpected difficulties as a wedding.

On the one hand, there is the high, nigh-unexplainable elation that two people have found each other and are declaring their eternal love for one another. On the other hand is the question of "Do we invite crazy Uncle Junior and loopy Aunt Penelope to the wedding?"

One the one hand, there is the simple and profound action of participating in a language event that actually performs what one says one is doing. ("I do" are not simply words that one mumbles but a promise that is seared into the living of our days by the mere utterance of words.) On the other hand, the "I do's" may be the only words that one remembers, as we all get lost in what Jesus cautioned against in his most famous sermon: "Worry not what we shall eat, and what we shall drink, and what shall we put on..."

Weddings are "purple paradoxes," meaning they are extraordinary occasions when the members of the wedding party are at once royalty in the eyes of their beloveds and as common, as daily, as familiar friends.

At any given congregation with a long history, it is amazing to imagine all the vows that have been spoken, the rings exchanged, the tears of joy and hope shared, not to mention the countless anxious, thrilled, and happy families and proud friends who have witnessed all those weddings.

Of course, what is most noteworthy are the lives that have been shaped as a result of all those weddings. The word "wedding" is a verb as well as a noun. The wedding ceremony is followed by a couple continuing to wed one another, again and again, on a daily basis, as they forge their future together.

Changes in careers, shifts in family locations, tragedies, and triumphs all work together to inspire and challenge a couple as the years deepen their commitment of love. What remains constant in an ever-growing marriage is the shining truth that the "wedding" is still going on.

Often a couple's future entails an ever-expanding family, as the gifts of children are added to life's equation. Then marriage takes on a decidedly different tone and tenor. As children leave the nest, a marriage experiences a new reality and a couple discovers a need to become wed in different ways.

Every noteworthy wedding, every exemplary marriage, in my experience, has contained certain qualities:

Love, obviously, is at the core of a lasting and fulfilling marriage. Love that's flexible and understanding, forgiving and faithful.

Commitment also must be part of each day in a marriage covenant. Some couples know the truth that William Willimon emphasizes about marriage: couple makes a promise, and then the promise makes the couple.

Hope is what inspires couples in their growing love, and it is what thrills the hearts of those who attend weddings and affirm the marriages they witness. We have good hopes of great things to come because of couples becoming married.

Joy is the culmination of the lifelong work of marriage, the theme for observing a wedding anniversary, the core of what human sharing is meant for, the gist of what the human heart is finally all about.

Jesus and the Crowds

> 1 When they had come near Jerusalem and had reached Bethphage, at the Mount of Olives, Jesus sent two disciples, 2 saying to them, "Go into the village ahead of you, and immediately you will find a donkey tied, and a colt with her; untie them and bring them to me. 3 If anyone says anything to you, just say this, "The Lord needs them." And he will send them immediately. 4 This took place to fulfill what had been spoken through the prophet, saying,
>
> 5 "Tell the daughter of Zion,
> Look, your king is coming to you,
> humble, and mounted on a donkey,
> and on a colt, the foal of a donkey."
>
> 6 The disciples went and did as Jesus had directed them; 7 they brought the donkey and the colt, and put their cloaks on them, and he sat on them. 8 A very large crowd spread their cloaks on the road, and others cut branches from the trees and spread them on the road. 9 The crowds that went ahead of him and that followed were shouting, "Hosanna to the Son of David! Blessed is the one who comes in the name of the Lord! Hosanna in the highest heaven!" (Matthew 21:1-9)

From the beginning of his three years of public ministry to the very end of his earthly life, Jesus was surrounded, accompanied, bothered, and blessed by crowds of people.

There was the hungry crowd — as all three of the synoptic gospels record the feeding of the five thousand — to which he had to respond, not only to the crowd's hunger but to the disciples' lack of imagination.

There was the desperate crowd (Matt. 13:2ff) so eager for a word of encouragement, so at-their-wits-end, so desperate, that they swarmed around Jesus to the point that he had to get into a boat and preach to them from the sea. There was the maimed, lame, and halt crowd, people who thronged around Jesus for his healing touch.

There was the lynching crowd at his hometown of Nazareth (Luke 4:16ff) that liked how he read Isaiah's prophecy (Is. 61) but didn't like how he interpreted the scriptural text in his sermon that followed and nearly resulted in his early execution.

Among the most famous of the crowds was the Palm Sunday Crowd — the lauding and applauding masses who had gathered in Jerusalem for the high festal occasion of Passover.

Food preparations were paramount.

Memories were stretching back all the way to the Hebrews' experience of bondage in Egypt, like ribbons of mental energy twisting and twining and weaving into a cord of recollection. One can't help but think that this was a time of family get-togethers, when families gathered from the far corners of the Galilean hillsides for their annual reunions.

And you can hear them remembering great songs of their faith, "Old #118," singing "Hosanna, hosanna, blessed is the one who comes in the name of the Lord."

What Jesus beheld on that first Palm Sunday is, I believe, pretty much what he'd behold today.

Crowds can certainly be feisty. But too soon they turn fickle. Crowds can be full of adulation, but they can quickly move toward abandonment. On Palm Sunday, Jesus heard the raucous acclaim of the crowds, but by Friday he would also hear their riotous demands for his head.

All of which is a cautionary tale about the wiles and ways of crowds:

1. *Be wary of any group that gives you too much credit* for something that God has had a hand in and others have contributed to.

2. *Don't despair too deeply if the crowds turn on you* and leave you out in the cold. It just may be that's when God will come to you, as God did to Jesus, in an especially new way.

3. *Be careful of joining too much in raucous crowds that reduce complex social problems to simplistic, mechanistic formulas.*

4. *Remember the crowd that God likes: the whole human family.* He desires a special relationship with each and every one of us, and not simply a select, darling few.

Augustine has it just right, as he describes how Jesus Christ loves all of us: *"He loves each and every one of us as if there were only one of us to love."*

Today, we are a crowd that Jesus loves very much. To avoid ever turning into a mob, or worse, an indifferent herd, let us realize how much God loves us and desires to meet us at this sacred table.

G.R.A.C.E.

Grace is all about **God** and the sacred intersection of Divine Drive and Humanity's Highway. God is the giver of grace — as the sun breaks at the new morning, in the midst of toil, when a difficult decision is finalized, in the caress of a parent on the cheek of a newborn child, when flowers open their blossoms to spring-time rain, whenever harmony is achieved between adversaries.

Grace is all about **Reconciliation**. Reconciliation in relationships, in our families, in our workplaces, among friends, even on the international scene. Is it not reconciling grace that has been a part of every peace agreement between former enemies? And don't we relish the possibilities for such graceful reconciliation when we strive for justice and goodness to prevail in our cities, our nation, our world?

Grace is an **Affirmation** by God. The grace we receive each and every day means that the world should continue toward betterment, fulfillment, and a more visible unity among all members of the human family. Holy, affirming grace is God's way of voting that the human enterprise should go on. Grace is God's hope-filled beckoning to us: "Come with me, this way."

Grace is all about **Celebration**. "When nothing else could help, love lifted me," goes an old, old hymn. The love of God can, and does, spark celebration in our hearts and even larger moments of in a congregation.

Grace is all about **Erasing**. Graceful "erasing" is at the core of God's intentions for humanity: to give us a second chance, to empower us for greater righteousness, to allow for another try at right actions, to make repentance a possibility. The erasing forgiveness for past mistakes, miscues, mishaps, and misdeeds.

G.R.O.W.T.H.

For individuals, groups, and institutions, growth is not only possible; it is a necessity. One of the fundamental wisdoms regarding all of life pertains directly to growth: if we do not grow, we wither and waste away. This coming week I urge you to consider the following "recipe for growth" for your life. Increase half of these ingredients in your life over the next seven days and see what happens to your general disposition and your overall well-being. Then try the other half and see how different your life is. My guess, based on observations of many people who are committed to personal growth, is that your present life and future prospects will dramatically increase. Let me know how your experiences with this "recipe" develop.

Gumption — An act of will, a specific decision, courage, bedrock commitment to your best purposes, determination — all these are synonymous with the colloquial term "gumption." Nothing significant is ever accomplished by human beings without it.

Renewal — The yearning to be renewed, the practice of being renewed on a regular basis, is always part of growth. Retreats, short getaways, taking a new way home, traveling to a place where they don't speak your language, plugging into a new adventure — all these (and more!) can enhance a sense of renewal in your spirit and thus contribute to growth.

Open Spirit — Maintaining an open spirit about others and yourself nearly always leads to deeper wisdom, fresh insights, and a calmer demeanor. Connecting with others with open spirits — like at church, particularly like at Community! — can multiply and magnify these same blessings.

Wide Vision — Of all the ingredients for growth, this one may be the most crucial one in groups and institutions. Where the vision is wide, our reach can be farther. Where the vision is wide, our understanding is deeper. Where the vision is wide, our love is enlarged beyond anything we dreamed possible.

Time — Like a savory wine, like the writing of a good novel, like the rebuilding of a football team, growth always requires time. Time to deepen and develop, time to stretch and strengthen, time to enhance and enlarge. A motto like "Time is of the essence" can certainly move us into action. But we also need to remember the psychotherapeutic adage: "Don't push the river."

Hopefulness — To grow in any way that is lasting and meaningful, hopefulness is an absolute must. Whether you maintain a posture of hopefulness by individual focus or by hooking up with a coach or by way of a covenant with an accountability partner or by involvement in a group, hope is a cornerstone of a fruitful, well-lived life. There is no substitute for hope in the overarching scheme of growth.

Hands on the Table

Nearly two thousand years after the first Lord's Supper, we still break the loaf and share the cup in remembrance of the One who let Himself be broken that we might be made whole. During the enriching rituals of Holy Week, real life is shared, actual agony is experienced, and the way is finally prepared for Jesus' crucifixion and resurrection.

Luke is alone among the gospels in telling of Jesus' after-dinner speech. A skilled writer, Luke sets up the disciples, and us 21st-century followers, by waiting until after the institution of the Lord's Supper to share a shocking revelation.

The subject of his after-dinner speech? Nothing comical, entertaining, or sentimental at all. It all focuses on betrayal.

About his betrayer Jesus says, "But see, the one who betrays me is with me, and his hand is on the table" (Luke 22:21).

These are hard words to hear. Hard, because they are so intimate: "with me." Hard, too, because they are so personal: "his hand." Hard, as well, because they are so insinuating: after Jesus' declaration about betrayal, the text says "they began to ask one another which one it could be who would do this."

But I suspect these words are hard for us to hear — as hard for us to hear as they were for the first disciples to hear — because they are also true, so applicably, directly true about all of Jesus' followers.

So let us do as Jesus suggested and see the hands on the table.

- Obviously, Jesus refers to Judas, for he is the one who will turn Jesus over to the authorities. Yet are there not other hands on the table, the hands of those who will also abandon Jesus in his time of need?
- See Peter's hand, apparently a strong hand, one that makes flamboyant gestures, yet it will shrink away in denial three times before the cock crows.
- See Thomas' hand, whose sense of touch is so acute that it will numb his heart's capacity to believe until he can actually put his hand into Jesus' wounds.

- See the bold and brazen hands of James and John who asked Jesus for the privilege of sitting in glory by his side, but who had no idea how to be disciples on a daily basis.
- See the weary hands of the disciples when they fail to remain steadfast as Jesus prays, when the time comes for Jesus' testing before public officials, as the crucifixion becomes excruciatingly real. Indeed, in other accounts of Jesus' final hours after the supper, he states that the disciples "will all fall away" and that they "will be scattered ... and leave me alone." And they did.

But we see other hands on the table as well. Anyone who breaks bread in remembrance of Jesus may ask, "What sort of hands do I bring to the Lord's table?"

- Some people have "overly pious" hands, so desperately clinging to heavenly religiosity that they can do no earthly good.
- Some people have "anti-praying" hands, so focused on the things of this world — and all of its attendant grime and grit and grunge — that they grow exhausted and dispirited because they have not taken enough time to be with God in quiet and stillness.
- Some people have "cynical, all-knowing, condescending" hands. With a flip of the wrist, some people dismiss the world's grossness, their leaders' grievous mistakes, and all untoward actions with a simple "Oh, I knew that. Yeah, I could have told you that would happen. They're all the same. It's all rotten, all the time."
- Some people have dominating "our-hands-are-the-best-kind-of-hands" hands, defined by the illusion of supremacy — by melanin content (or lack thereof), or by wrinkles and age-spots (or lack thereof), denying all the while the truth on which Paul and the members of the early Church would stake their lives, that in Christ we are all one.

- On yet another hand, some people have "indifferent" hands, overestimating the power of the shadowy places in the world, and underestimating their own God-given capacities, turning away from the world, and often their lives, with a "Woe-is-me-what-can-one-person-do?" shrug of their souls. And when they — when *we* — do this, we neglect Christ's daring invitation to grasp the illuminating power of goodness and hope.

Now, before we grow despondent, please know there is good news about all this "hands" business. Yes, we agree that Jesus refers to Judas' betraying hands, and Peter's and Thomas' and the rest of the disciples' hands, and also our own hands. But let us also remember one other fact. All those hands, all our hands, are not set forth on the Lord's Table alone.

Remember, remember, remember — for remembering is what the Lord's Supper is for — our hands are on the table with His hands. While our hands can betray and doubt and be overly pious and anti-prayer and cynical and exclusive and indifferent, Christ's hands are there for us. As Jesus was "the man for others," as Bonhoeffer would describe him, His hands are for us. And how wondrous those hands are: healing hands, hoping hands, honoring hands, forgiving hands, encouraging hands. Hands of generosity and welcome, hands of hospitality and justice, hands of grace and faithfulness.

So faithful are Christ's hands that we come to a new understanding of the phrase "saved by faith": we are saved by God's faith, by God's continuously renewing, resurrecting faith in His children. And God in Christ offers his saving hands on the Table with an ultimate purpose and hope.

As Christ's hands overcome excruciating loss and pain, so shall ours.

As Christ's hands triumphed over the world's detractors, so shall ours.

As Christ's hands rose in resurrecting power to bless the world once more, so shall ours. Thanks be to God for Christ's hands — pierced and crucified and resurrected — which redeem all the other hands on the table.

Prayer: We give you thanks, O God, for the broken loaf that makes us whole, for the shared cup that fills us to completeness, for accepting us as we are, hands and all.

AMEN.

Doxologies

When and where was the last time you sang a doxology? Every week millions upon millions of Christians sing it in worship, usually after receiving the offering. They join in offering musical thanks to God for the plenty they have received. Some sing loud, some sing demurely.

Such thanks are offered because, usually, it seems natural to do so. Some folks participate in the doxology because they think they ought to; it's plainly the decent thing to do in polite Christian circles.

Some folks sing or say the doxology because of an overwhelming humility or the rush of joy or the thrill of exaltation.

It is safe to say that around the world, in countless congregations, somewhere, somehow, someone is offering a doxology each and every Sunday of the year.

But expressions of gratitude through the doxology need not be limited to Sunday mornings or Wednesday evenings or other times of "official" worship. Indeed, the plentitude of graces supplied by God behooves us to be about the business of singing doxologies on numerous occasions outside our gathered worship experiences.

Consider now those times when you have been singing a doxology. What occasions prompted your offering of thanks? Did something in the natural realm cause you joyous awe? Was it something a child said or did? Was your doxological moment stimulated by a task completed or by an unexpected gift or by a surprise visit from an engaging stranger?

Did you use the words of the traditional Sunday morning doxology ("Praise God from whom all blessings flow...")? Or did you have another set of words or another tune in your heart and on your lips at the time?

Did others join you for a hearty refrain of thanksgiving? Or was yours a quiet sort of doxology, offered, say, in the solitude of your car or along the exercise path or even down the aisle at the grocery store?

The singing of doxologies need not be restricted to weekly worship in the gathered community of faith. Doxologies can and do go on all the time in the expressions of gratitude of the faithful everywhere.

One truth is made consistently plain in our journey in God's grace: *all occasions can inspire us to sing a doxology.*

Whether changing a diaper, or walking the dog, or doing our jobs, or preparing a meal, or attending a concert, or sitting in on a class, or digging in the garden, or paying the bills, or reading the Bible, or writing a note, or watching a movie, or following the news, or holding a hand, or passing along a communion tray, or tasting a peach, or smelling a rose, or beholding a sunset, or listening to the rain, the truth abides: *now is the time to sing the doxology.*

ns:
20 QUESTIONS:
A VOICE OF FAITH ANSWERS IN THE PUBLIC SQUARE

All You Need Is More Love

"What are the best and worst examples of parenting in the Bible?"

For Christians and Jews, and for a considerable portion of Western culture, the Bible is like a family album, portraying the best and worst examples of what human beings are capable of doing to one another.

Among the worst examples of parenting in the Bible are Eli (sacrificing one's family for work), Isaac and Rebekah (playing favorites among their children) and Lot (pimping his daughters).

Still, I would nominate as "worst" the parents who lead the "Whoever" family, as Jesus cautions in Matthew 18:6: "But whoever causes one of these little ones who believe in me to sin ..."

Directly provoking children to intentional wrongdoing can scar them for life and condemn them to a future fraught with defeat, discouragement, and despair. Such a caution is good not only in the biblical context but is relevant and applies to all of us in contemporary life.

One of the best — if not the best — parenting examples can be found in Luke 15:11-32, in the provocative account of "The Loving Father" who treats his wastrel youngest son and his self-righteous older son with exceeding grace and generosity.

He is really the "prodigal" — that word can mean extravagant and liberal, as well as wasteful or reckless — one in Jesus' parable, meeting each of his sons with overwhelming love and forgiveness.

The father of the parable provides an ideal example, however challenging, for us to follow. From a parent's point of view, this can be an extraordinarily difficult standard to meet.

But from a child's point of view, who wouldn't want such a parent?

"What if I'm not certain about what I believe?"

To cling to absolute certainty about what one believes about God can border on idolatry.

In the end, God is a dynamic mystery, and we are wise to clothe our beliefs in an attitude of humility whenever we approach the intersection of divinity and humanity.

If you're uncertain, that's OK. And it's OK to share your uncertainty. Our nation's public discourse (including conversations about religion and culture) would be much more civil and inspirational if more of us would admit, on occasion, "I don't know."

Trust and confidence are better strategies than certainty for belief and faith, because they're not normally derailed by questions and doubts. Questions and doubts can, in fact, keep our faith vibrantly alive and open to the light of new knowledge.

Trust and confidence were supremely evident in Jesus' life and among his followers.

The Gospel of Mark records Jesus teaching about belief as he encounters a boy possessed by an unclean spirit. In the midst of Jesus' healing of the boy, the boy's father proclaims, "I believe, help my unbelief."

As we seek clarity about what we believe, three things are paramount — we are all "works in process"; sacred texts and holy traditions provide great examples of how to grow in faith; believing is developed best in a faith community where questions are welcomed and loving God and neighbor are encouraged as the best ways to live.

And remember Gracie Allen's famous declaration, "Never place a period where God has placed a comma."

"Does God hear the prayers of nonbelievers?"

A treasured phrase in the prophet Joel — echoed in an epistle of the Apostle Paul — describes how "Everyone who calls on the name of the Lord shall be saved." That declaration intimates that God is ever ready to be in relationship with every human being.

Any religion that excludes non-adherents from God's love and merciful care borders on committing the sin of arrogance. How presumptuous to limit God's magnanimous grace and eternal love.

Of course, certain religions condone, promote, and practice an exclusivistic understanding of God and how God relates to human beings. But in the end, to paraphrase Browning, their reach exceeds their grasp, and, as Jesus put it, they know not what they are doing.

The most exemplary followers within all religions assume a posture of humility before God and generosity toward anyone seeking God's guidance, help, and reception of their prayers.

Now, if God hears all prayers, one can wonder about prayers that arise out of derelict desires and malevolent intentions. Surely we can trust God's magisterial wisdom and everlasting justice to deny any curse upon an elected official, any death-wish for a political leader, any condemnation of a celebrity.

Instead of worrying about whose prayers God hears, it behooves all persons to pray for a more sensitive union with our Creator, an increase of comity and good will with others, and a closer fidelity with the "better angels of our nature." The rest we can leave in God's hands.

"How far should Christian tolerance of other faiths go?"

Among the causes of bloodshed and suffering in human history, religious intolerance ranks near the top of the list. If we want a future different from the past, we will be acutely sensitive toward those who treasure a faith different from our own.

To practice tolerance is not to engage in acceptance, but rather respect — to offer the same respect towards others that one yearns for oneself.

Christianity honors the practice of tolerance: "For whoever does the will of my Father in heaven is my brother and sister and mother" (Matthew 12:50).

Jesus consistently practiced revolutionary tolerance towards those who possessed religious status different from his own. He reserved his harshest critiques and challenges for those within his own camp.

There are adherents in every faith who demand that the faith expressions of others are inferior. Such demands are of human, not divine, origin. In fact, such demands amount to rationalizations for spiritual annihilation. No religion is worth having if it requires the deaths of all other religions.

Pope John XXIII once offered a great, saving adage: "Let us look at each other without mistrust, meet each other without fear, and talk with each other without surrendering principle."

Living up to such high ideals will help to create a world where not only are differing faiths tolerated but the unity of peace is celebrated.

"Where is the irony in the gospels?"

Irony is a literary strategy involving wordplay, double entendre, sarcasm or dramatic reversal. In narrative, irony functions disruptively, overturning the applecart of our anticipations, upsetting our usual understandings of situations, characters in a story, and worldviews. Numerous instances of irony emerge in the New Testament. "For those who want to save their life will lose it" (Luke 9:24). "So the last will be first" (Matthew 20:16). "The stone that was rejected by ... the builders ... has become the cornerstone" (Acts 4:11). Through such ironic declarations, new worlds of possibility are opened to those with ears (and hearts) to receive them.

While the famous parable of the Good Samaritan (Luke 10:25-37) may seem, to current sensibilities, a moral directive — "Go and do likewise" — its greater power is found in its irony. The lawyer whose questions would test Jesus is himself tested by Jesus. Those who would trap Jesus are themselves cornered into recognizing that a new master teacher has come to town.

Jesus answers the lawyer's question ("And who is my neighbor?") by telling a story about a man who falls among robbers along the Jericho road. No one helps the man except a Samaritan who is moved by compassion.

Jesus' original hearers would not have expected a hated enemy like a Samaritan to arise as the hero of any tale. They would have been hard-pressed even to put the words "good" and "Samaritan" together. Through such tension, however, the parable functions to reshape how we expect neighbors to act and be.

A larger question for religious practitioners today is this: If the parable in Luke 10 were contemporized, which surprising character or group would we be hard pressed to call "good"?

"What are we to make of the three versions of Jesus' 'last words'?"

The New Testament gospel narratives contain what are traditionally regarded as the "Seven Last Words of Christ." Uttered in the harrowing anguish of the crucifixion, they are among the most inspirational of Jesus' proclamations, each one of them a veritable sermon. Luke's gospel contains three of these traditional "last words," while John's gospel has three different ones, and Matthew bears one more.

Matthew's "last word" has Jesus quoting from Psalm 22: *My God, my God, why have you forsaken me?* Down through the centuries countless people have found comfort in the notion that Jesus could experience and express utter abandonment. Accordingly, all prayers, especially honest anguish, establish connections to one's ultimate source.

John's brief "last word" — *It is finished* — can be understood as a searing truth about his earthly life and the initiation of his mission. Christ was finished with the world's haughty attempt at humiliation, finished with the world's vain attempt to keep him in its grasp and control his gospel of radical grace. His movement of care, compassion, justice, mercy, welcome, and wonder was now launched.

According to Luke's gospel, the light of day was eclipsed as Jesus, the one proclaimed as "the light of the world," illuminated the central thesis of his entire ministry: *Father, unto thy hands I commend my spirit.* No despairing submission. No bitter resignation. Simply and finally trusting surrender into the grace-filled hands of God. Who else but God would have hands strong enough to receive the rabbi carpenter's spirit?

These three "last words" are invitations to honest anguish, acknowledgement that Jesus' mission has been launched, and trusting in the ultimate grace of God.

"Do you see any prophecies that are coming true today?"

There are prophecies, and then there are prophecies.

I am among those who take the Bible far too seriously to take it literally.

Therefore, what some people see as definitive predictions of actual historical events coming true in the present (or near future), I would see as prophetic calls, uttered to inspire people to action and justice. For example, when the prophet Amos proclaims, "Let justice roll down like waters, and righteousness like an ever-flowing stream," he is issuing a clarion invitation for us to participate in justice and righteousness.

As we help justice become real, such prophecies become fulfilled. Dr. King and the cause of civil rights he advocated were supreme examples of such a prophecy "coming true." Or, when the prophet Joel proclaims, "Your old men shall dream dreams, and your young men shall see visions," he is proffering the visionary hope of what happens when God's Spirit infuses lives with purpose and courage.

Have we witnessed such dreaming and envisioning? You bet. But no one can ever tell exactly when or where such events will take place. Our sacred texts, our wisest scholars, our capacities of reason, and our own experiences work together to determine how prophecies become realities. But no one can ever really predict the future.

Crystal balls are surely entertaining diversions. But prophecies have always been intended for the strengthening of faith.

"What can mainline denominations do about the rising number of 'nones,' as in people who claim no faith?"

In light of recent research on the increase of Americans claiming no religious affiliation, mainline denominations can do much better what they have done somewhat poorly in the past, namely offering: (1) caring affirmation, (2) clarifying questions, (3) enthusiastic welcome, and (4) innovative, authentic ways of "being church."

Even though "nones" may eschew the trappings of religious institutions, they are not unlike everyone else: ever in need of the love and care of God and the gifts of community. Mainline denominations have a long-standing regard for humanity and God's care for the world. But they must show forth a compelling alternative to popular caricatures of religion as a fount of condemnation.

To those who are resistant to any religious belief whatsoever, mainline denominations have the royal opportunity to offer an engaging invitation: "Tell me what kind of God you don't believe in. I just might not believe in that notion of God either. Would you be open to thinking about and experiencing God in a new way?"

Some churches seem to have lowered their "ecclesial thermostats" to freezing, particularly on Sundays. Mainline denominations can heighten their engagement with the unaffiliated by offering warm hospitality and welcome to strangers, visitors, and even their own members.

Mainline denominations can also begin to offer more creative presentations of their liturgy and Bible studies, and to re-think their "outreach mission" — not as member recruitment but as innovative, caring service to others. The key, always, with "nones" as with all others, is authenticity.

"What about the sick and maimed animals in Malachi?"

To better understand the book of the prophet Malachi, it's best to know something about ritual practices in his day.

Malachi, whose name means "Messenger," proffered his prophetic declarations sometime between 445 and 432 BCE. At that time, ritual sacrifice was understood by the Hebrew people to be a pleasing and mandated way to worship God. For selfish reasons, however, the best animals, which ritual tradition required be sacrificed, were instead withheld.

Very few, if any, faith groups would entertain such a practice today. But that's beside the point. There is a powerful metaphorical lesson at work in Malachi.

Proper worship practices, proper use of our resources, and proper responses of gratitude to God have always been of ultimate concern to the Hebrew people and the God of the Bible. This is the gist of Malachi's complaint in the first chapter of the book that bears his name.

Instead of showing righteousness, the people "profaned" their relationship with God. The table of God's welcome has been "polluted," and some folks are called out-and-out "cheats." The people are neither doing nor giving their best.

Which could be a fair critique in some communities of faith, especially those that place their own satisfaction above the welfare and fulfillment of those in need.

This not-giving-our-best also applies when any religious group settles for less, intellectually. When we don't exercise our mental capacities, we fail to abide by the great commandment to "Love the Lord your God with all your heart and with all your soul and with all your *mind*."

In order not to cheat God — or ourselves — Malachi reminds us to bring our best selves before the throne of God's grace — especially when it can help another — and never save what's best for later. As Annie Dillard has said, "Give it all, give it now."

"What does your faith say about living in the moment?"

In the Christian tradition, Jesus' most famous oration, the Sermon on the Mount, contains a clarion call for living in the moment: "So do not worry about tomorrow. ... Today's trouble is enough for today."

Not that Jesus disdained the past. To the contrary, Jesus honored his Jewish heritage again and again, keeping the commandments, practicing time-honored prayer rituals, and treasuring the words of scripture, especially the Psalms and the prophets.

Nor did he dismiss the future as insignificant. Jesus regularly urged his followers to be prepared and hopeful in the face of the future, as the apostle Paul also did with the early Christians.

But Jesus' preponderant emphasis was on current righteousness and an awareness of God's present nearness.

The Bible consistently exhibits a fondness for the present moment. In the New Testament, "today" is used three times as often as "tomorrow" and ten times as often as "yesterday." According to Luke's gospel, Jesus' first sermon, in his hometown of Nazareth, began with the word "Today."

Focusing on living in the moment helps us to avoid languishing in nostalgia for a sentimentalized (and perhaps fictional) past as well as adoring some idealized fanciful future.

And while memory is always instructive, and anticipation always energizes action, the path for an ultimately invigorating and life-giving faith follows the beckoning path of the present.

I believe Jesus would agree with E.L. Doctorow's wise counsel: "You can only see as far as your headlights, but you can make the whole trip that way."

"What do you think Jesus is up to?"

The spirit and presence of Jesus abides among his followers. In connections wrought by prayer, in rituals remembering his resurrecting love, in actions embodying his ideals, in study over his teachings, Jesus is there.

Jesus' presence is made real in families and congregations, giving purpose and direction to those at the beginning of life.

For followers at the end of life, Jesus promises to come and take them unto himself with a blessing of eternal companionship (John 14:3).

For those devastated by disaster and destruction, Jesus' heart is the first of all hearts to break.

For those yearning for peace to prevail over strife and war, Jesus is there in the imagination of those who plan projects and give witness to better ways of living.

Jesus' presence is made real whenever anyone senses an injustice or a deficit in the human community, particularly among those with whom he ultimately identified: "Truly I tell you, just as you did it to one of the least of these who are members of my family, you did it to me" (Matthew 25:40).

In John Steinbeck's Pulitzer-winning novel *The Grapes of Wrath*, Tom Joad echoes that solidarity: "I'll be all around in the dark — I'll be everywhere. Wherever you can look — wherever there's a fight, so hungry people can eat, I'll be there. ... I'll be in the way kids laugh when they're hungry and they know supper's ready."

In mysterious and strange ways, Jesus is providing encouragement and compassion in a manner that eludes final definition. In other, equally wondrous ways, what Jesus is up to, is up to those who live his way of life.

"How do I use my faith to learn to forgive?"

All who ask this question and earnestly seek answers to it are already on the way to acquiring life-saving learning about forgiveness and wholeness.

Becoming better acquainted with your faith's scriptures, prayers, and rituals will result in exciting insights and a powerful impact on your life.

Reading scripture can remind you of forebears who have been where you are now. A regular, disciplined recitation of prayers can provide peace and confidence to aid in the challenging work of forgiveness. Participating in forgiveness rituals (annually or weekly) can shape your life with hope and grace.

Of course, faith is always lived out best in community. If you have a faith home, seek the guidance of your leaders. If you don't currently have a faith community, ask a friend who exemplifies a forgiving spirit about their place of worship and join them for a service or a study group.

As we probe sacred texts, special prayers, cherished rituals, and the life of a faith community, one thing becomes clear: we are best fulfilled as human beings when we learn how to give and receive forgiveness. Christianity's most famous prayer, the Lord's Prayer, describes forgiveness as a two-way street: "Forgive us our trespasses (sins), as we forgive those who trespass (sin) against us."

And always remember: forgiveness is the supreme antidote to the harsh and destructive impossibility of perfectionism. At the root of all worthy religions is a precious proposition: there is always more merciful forgiveness in God than there are misdeeds in us.

"Will fasting improve my faith life?"

The time-tested practice of fasting can certainly enhance your faith life if you approach it with humility and clarity of purpose.

We normally think of fasting as abstention from food and drink. It is that, of course, but it is so much more. All monotheistic faith traditions (Judaism, Christianity, Islam) include it as a spiritual discipline. Countless other religions (including Hinduism, Buddhism and Taosim) also encourage fasting.

Fasting is not for everybody. An inventory of one's motives for fasting is in order. (And those on prescribed diets or nutrition regimens should consult their doctors.)

If we fast as a method of denigrating the body in order to leverage favor with the Divine, we twist the essential purposes of fasting. If we fast as a kind of sanctified weight-loss program or bodily detoxification, we cheapen the spiritual blessings available through fasting.

Fasting has to do with paying attention — less attention to things that are ephemeral and more attention to aspects of life that are ultimately valuable.

Fasting is done best within a faith community, under a religious leader's guidance, with readings and times of prayer before, during and after the fast, and a temporary restructuring of one's normal schedule.

Abstaining from what we normally consume can help us realize that we are not merely consumers. Instead, fasting can confirm the invigorating truth that we are precious creations of a Creator who yearns for loving relationships with us all and for just, compassionate relations among all human beings.

"If you could celebrate Christmas in a different country, which would it be?"

To celebrate Christmas in a land other than one's own is extraordinarily hard to fathom, given the powerful attachments of sentiment, custom, family, friends, and beautifully particular, home-specific rituals.

But worse still would be not trying to imagine the Yuletide gifts and graces of other locales. Christmas always holds more wondrous blessings than any one place can contain.

Mexico would certainly be one of the places where my soul could find spiritual nourishment at Christmastime. The tradition of "Las Posadas," a nine-day festival portraying the Holy Family seeking shelter and being turned away in one place after another, shows God's indefatigable spirit, which will be undeterred until humanity finally receives the divine gift of incarnational love.

England also attracts my fancy, since its genius musicians originated some of the most beloved Christmas compositions. Wesley and Handel, alone, distinguish Britain as a Christmas-music epicenter.

Italy pulls equally strongly on my Christmas heartstrings because of St. Francis' holy audacity in creating what is understood to have been the first "Living Nativity" scene.

But this Christmas perhaps it is Egypt that has a special allure for me, and possibly many others. For it was in Egypt, according to the gospel of Matthew, that Mary, Joseph, and baby Jesus, refugees all, found safe harbor in a brutish and brutalizing world.

Two millennia later, could Christians, especially those of us in the U.S., learn key, saving lessons about the Christmas spirit and the essence of holy hospitality from our ancient, non-Christian, Egyptian exemplars?

"When does something in my life become a 'false god'?"

A "false god" is any lie, any deception, any idol which we allow to occupy the place, position, and status of God in our lives.

Whenever we offer our utmost trust or allegiance to something other than our Creator — to possessions, to money, to guns, to a movement, to a group, to an idea — we commit idolatry and worship a "false god."

Whenever insecurities, anxiousness, and fears prevail in our thoughts and deeds, "false gods" are near.

Whenever we make compromises with difficult truths, settle for deceptions, engage with life's predicaments with willful ignorance, we succumb to "false gods."

Whenever we render the mystery of the Divine completely comprehensible, we even make God into a "false god." God's majesty and glory always exceed our grasp.

The Bible is replete with evidence that even the most well-intentioned people can, and regularly do, chase after "false gods." The testimony of the Hebrew prophets, the proclamations of Jesus, and the witness of the early Church sound the alarm about such idolatry.

And the human saga is soaked with the blood of untold millions who suffered from fascistic leaders (and their maniacal followers) whose chasing after "false gods" resulted in history's greatest tragedies, including Auschwitz, Cambodia's killing fields, Soviet gulags, the Middle Passage, the Trail of Tears, and Boko Haram's butchery, to mention just a few.

The key to answering the question lies in the word "something." Anything can become a "false god." Humble, fierce, honest, persistent wrestling with life's situations can definitely help us resist "false gods."

"Should I read sacred texts of a faith that's not my own?"

The simple answer is "Yes." For any person yearning to live a truly relevant and authentic faith in an ever-changing world, the answer is "Absolutely Yes!"

Some people may regard reading sacred texts of other religions as potentially damaging. But such thinking borders on superstition.

How poor would be our faith and how weak our understanding of our own tradition, whether we were a Muslim threatened by reading the gospel of John, or a Christian threatened by the thought of perusing the *Bhagavad Gita*, or a Hindu threatened by exploring the soaring rhetoric of the prophet Isaiah.

We are impoverished if the only sacred texts we read are those of our own faith. Reading the holy books of religions other than one's own expands one's worldview with surprising insights. For example, when Christians read the Qur'an, they discover that Mary, Jesus' mother, is cited there more than in all the New Testament documents combined. Further research reveals that Muslims, particularly in Turkey, highly venerate Mary.

For Christians, the Hebrew Bible — what is commonly called the "Old Testament" — is not only recommended but essential reading for a fulfilling faith. The Psalms were Jesus' prayerbook, and he continually referenced psalms and the prophets throughout his ministry.

Sacred texts are the cornerstones of every religion worthy of adherence. And understanding the sacred texts of others is a cornerstone for a saner and safer world.

"Does everyone have a guardian angel, even bad people?"

Portrayed and praised in the Hebrew Bible and the New Testament, theologically proclaimed by Jerome and Honorius of Autun, guardian angels are affirmed by Jewish, Catholic, Orthodox, Protestant, Muslim, and Zoroastrian traditions.

Whether they're piously described as "ministering spirits" (Hebrews 1:14) or affectionately depicted like George Bailey's angelic aide Clarence in the movie *It's A Wonderful Life*, guardian angels provide hopeful assistance in unaccountable ways and in the most unexpected moments.

A truth underpinning the experiences we describe with the term "guardian angel" is this: We are not alone in our struggles. We have help from beyond.

Sometimes such help is wondrously manifested in encounters we can't rationally explain. Sometimes such help is mysteriously conveyed through the hands and hearts of those we meet in the flesh.

A corollary truth is this: Whether we recognize it or not, God wills good for all human beings.

The key, of course, is whether we will welcome the help and the holy intention, a prerogative which is for each person to exercise, or not.

A third, crucial underpinning is this: Guardian angels are not merely extensions of our will, doing what human beings want, fetching us what we desire, accommodating our every manipulation.

Rather, they remind us of the best in ourselves and in others, even when we have forgotten that we or anyone else ever had a best self. In this sense especially, even the most hard-hearted can receive angelic help. Good or bad, what is required is to humbly acknowledge one's own neediness.

"Will faith and prayer help finally feed all the poor?"

Faith and prayer are the heart-and-soul dynamics motivating many a hand to feed the poor. The seeming intractability of poverty and hunger can certainly weary the spirit. But the sacred blessings of food — for hunger's satisfaction, proper nutrition (especially for children), and caring fellowship — can also inspire those who pray to embody acts of compassion.

Let us remember that countless food pantries and soup kitchens have been established by religious individuals and communities. Relief agencies like Bread for the World, Heifer International, and the Salvation Army were likewise founded by countless faithful folks.

Faith and prayers by themselves, however, have never filled anyone's belly. The New Testament book of James offers a summary critique for those engaged in "talking the talk" without "walking the walk": "If a brother or sister is ill-clad and in lack of daily food, and one of you says to them, 'Go in peace, be warmed and filled,' without giving them the things needed for the body, what does it profit? So faith by itself, if it has no works, is dead."

Thus, a crucial calculus abides between a faith of integrity and feeding the poor. A poignant prayer from Latin America can serve as a model petition for us all: "O God, to those who have hunger, give bread; and to those who have bread, give a hunger for justice."

With such a prayer — and sufficient time and imagination — it is feasible that all the poor could be fed, both here and around the world.

"What's your bucket list for Christians? In other words, what do you think a believer should do before they die?"

"Bucket lists" — sets of actions or experiences which people hope to fulfill before they die — are endlessly wondrous and intriguing: visit every major league baseball park; learn to cook crawfish etouffée; read all of Alice Walker's writings; travel to Tierra del Fuego; dance with each of your children at their weddings; and on and on.

Such lists for religiously and spiritually inclined folks often focus on global holy places like Jerusalem, Rome, Mecca, Lambini, the Ganges River. Others center on the birthplaces of founders and exemplary leaders in one's tradition.

A bucket list for Christians needs to be fashioned individually, with an eye toward personal fulfillment and compassionate care for others. Surely some of the following would qualify as bucket list items:

- Say thanks to those who have contributed the most to your life and faith.
- Discover the holy places (akin to Bethlehem and Sinai) wherever you live.
- Attend a worship service of a faith different than your own.
- Read through the entire Bible, at least once, applying lessons learned from it along the way.
- Participate in a mission trip.
- Share communion in another country.
- Make friends with your biggest doubt.
- Experience one moment of pure, focused attention on the sheer presence of God.

The best attitude for constructing such a list is to consider it not as an obligation but as an adventurous opportunity to gain deeper connections with God, one's faith traditions, and the human family.

Begin today, even if you're years away from kicking the bucket.

Big Questions at UMKC

Last week I had the great privilege of gathering with some UMKC students for a dialogue about "Big Questions." I was part of a four-person interfaith panel asked to address several truly "big" questions:

- What is the essence of your religion in a nutshell?
- What is the meaning of life? Why are we here?
- What happens when we die?
- Where does evil come from?

No shallow-end-of-the-pool questions for the UMKC crowd!

The questions generated among the students in response to our presentations were impressive and remarkably thought-provoking, artful, honest, and occasionally even daring.

The discussion was considerate and substantial. References to Moses, Buddha, meta-ethics, the meta-narrative of Western civilization, Shakespeare, Schweitzer, Solomon, and John Wesley suffused the room's atmosphere.

I came away from the evening with a strengthened hope for us all, thinking to myself, "We're making real progress, yes we are! The future is promising, with minds like these engaged in questions like those!"

If you ever grow discouraged about the human prospect, I encourage you to check out the "Big Questions" discussion group that meets in the community room at 5051 Oak St.

LETTERS TO FAMILY IN A TIME OF TURMOIL & TORMENT

Love is patient; love is kind; love is not jealous or boastful; it is not arrogant or rude. Love does not insist on its own way; it is not irritable or resentful; it does not rejoice in wrong-doing, but rejoices in the truth. (I Corinthians 13:4-6)

When life presents circumstances, situations, and predicaments that are not loving — when cruelty rears its head, when envy and narcissism supplant peaceableness, when pride and insolent discourtesy seek to usurp humility and common decency, when belligerence is exalted over cooperation, when resentment becomes weaponized, when objective facts and truth-telling are assaulted by key leaders of one's nation — one should speak up.

And so, over the course of eighteen months, I wrote three letters to my dear nephews and niece as a way of loving them and as a way of loving the people, the land, and the democracy we share as citizens of the United States of America.

Election Eve — November 7, 2016

Dear Christopher, Matthew, Nicholas, Catherine, and Lincoln,

On the eve of our national election tomorrow, I'm writing to share with you the presidential candidate for whom I will cast my vote.

Because of the work I've been doing with What U Can Do — a new 501(c)3 organization focused over the past 11 months on voter registration, voter education, and voter turnout — I have had to be publicly silent and necessarily nonpartisan about all candidates — national, state, and local — during the primary and general election campaigns.

As I believe you know by now, I'm not a person who is averse to a good struggle, a hefty debate, or a difficult discussion. But even though I am now Community's Minister Emeritus and thus no longer bound to public neutrality regarding candidates running for public office, including those running for the office of president, I have restrained my tongue and muted my opinions in the public square.

This intentional quieting — on Facebook, on my Google account, in newspaper articles, in public appearances on radio and television around Kansas City — was done in order to preserve the integrity of What U Can Do's work and strengthen our growing reputation as an organization concerned about the welfare of all people.

It was also done for the purpose of maintaining a capacity for "speaking truth to power" when or if the need arose. (A rule of thumb for clergy dictates that it's hard, sometimes even impossible, to maintain a prophetic edge in one's public discourse if one advocates publicly — or is perceived to be — too much on one candidate's or party's side.)

This evening I want you to know who I will be voting for tomorrow, and why. I don't want the next generation in our family ever to think that I avoided taking a stand in a moment of crisis. I don't want any of you ever to think I shirked the responsibility of stating my preferences during what will likely go down in history as one of the most tumultuous political moments and possibly the most consequential election our country has endured in a long, long time.

Tomorrow I will vote for Hillary Clinton for president.

I believe she has a keen mind — sharp enough to grapple with the legion of problems we will face as a nation in the near and far future. I believe she possesses a heart compassionate enough to embrace all citizens and those who yearn to bear that noble title. I believe she has a soul deep and tender enough to humble herself even while president and to lean upon the divine dimension in her life and the wise counsel of those who would surround her as part of a presidential team.

I also believe she has weathered a toxic storm of criticism and a tsunami of assaults lasting for more than a quarter of a century. She has certainly proven her mettle by rising triumphantly in the face of attacks that would have withered lesser leaders.

If she is elected, she will need the strength she has garnered over the broad reach of her public service to help build credibility in her proposed administration and to bring healing to the American body politic. Goodness knows she has been steeled and toughened up enough to do that.

Furthermore, I believe Hillary Clinton would be a far superior president than Donald Trump. To me, Hillary Clinton is to Donald Trump as a Pulitzer Prize-winning novel is to a bad cartoon, as steel is to papier-mâché, as the Gulf of Mexico is to a mud puddle. While he may feign otherwise, Donald Trump can't carry Hillary Clinton's luggage when it comes to being a vessel of gravitas, grit, and grace in fulfilling the duties of the presidency.

In truth, I'm embarrassed, ashamed even, that a major political party in our country would produce a nominee like Donald Trump.

This shame is a real feeling, even though I am not and never have been a member of the Republican Party. To be sure, Hillary Clinton is an imperfect candidate herself, with plenty of barnacles on her political ship. She has erred, missed the mark, and failed, sometimes miserably.

But she's not an embarrassment, a pathetic sham, a joke as a candidate.

From a certain angle, Donald Trump seems the natural product of a troubling evolution within the Republican Party. Starting with the cynical, opportunistic welcoming of Strom Thurmond and the rest of the Dixiecrats, and then the bigoted countenancing of the racist fringe of the South (and North), and then the accommodating of the "religious right" into the very center of the Republican tent, and then the sharing of power with the obstructionist Tea Party, the Republican Party has made a huge pot of trouble for itself. Rather than a coalition, it has become a contemptible cauldron of septic resistance and destructive skepticism, hardly recognizable as "the party of Lincoln."

During this year's campaigns, Donald Trump has distinguished himself not only as a dastardly candidate for the Republicans, but also one of the most repugnant candidates in the history of American politics. He has revealed himself to be a deceitful, fact-averse, insulting, misogynistic, xenophobic, homophobic, belligerent bully.

A side note: this past summer I asked a journalist friend here in Kansas City for counsel. He is one of the wisest persons of faith I know, with a steady gaze on history and its often wrenching, painful turnings.

I was so concerned about the fascistic leanings of Trump's candidacy that I wondered out loud if a movement of faith leaders should create a new "Barmen Declaration," parallel to the document adopted in 1934 by certain German Christians in light of the "Nazification" of Germany, including its churches and cultural life.

I was not unaware that the Barmen Declaration came "too late," since by the time it was composed and released Hitler and his followers, aided and abetted by his most loyal minion Joseph Goebbels, had effectively "conquered" Germany. I wondered if a similar declaration could preemptively help to staunch a rise of fascism in the U.S.

I wonder about that still, but I do not worry. For while no country is ever perfect, and we always need to be vigilant about the rise of bigotry and prejudice as political weapons, I believe, with Abraham Lincoln, that "the better angels of our nature" will somehow prevail in America.

The list of insults and degradations Donald Trump has offered during his primary and general election campaigns will fill forthcoming history books to overflowing:

- calling Senator John McCain a loser and besmirching his service to our country, disparaging his experiences as a POW;
- calling Mexicans "criminals ... and rapists";
- claiming that thousands of Muslims in New Jersey cheered the destruction of the Twin Towers;
- denigrating Megyn Kelly by saying she had blood coming out of "wherever";
- referring to Elizabeth Warren as "Pocahontas";
- belittling democracy and refusing to honor historically sanctified American traditions regarding "the peaceful transfer of power";
- inciting an environment of toxicity and violence among followers;
- mocking a handicapped reporter;
- denigrating the Khans, a Gold Star family, even to the point of insinuating that Mrs. Khan wasn't allowed by her Muslim faith to speak at the Democratic Convention;
- ridiculously claiming that he knows more about ISIS than U.S. military generals;
- advocating waterboarding and other methods of torture;
- despising Hillary Clinton to the point of insinuating that she lacks the stamina to perform the duties of the presidential office;
- blowing racist "dog-whistles" about places like Philadelphia and St. Louis "stealing" the election from him;
- describing Carly Fiorina as having an "unelectable" face;
- calling for the building of a fence to keep immigrants out of "our" country;
- suggesting a ban on all Muslims;

- belittling Purple Heart recipients and other soldiers by describing how he "always wanted one," as if a Purple Heart was something one could willfully obtain;
- intoning a spiteful rhetoric of vitriol toward anyone who chooses to disagree with him;
- expressing megalomaniacal self-delusion about himself as the only person who can fix America's problems;
- refusing to release his taxes;
- lying about his donations to veterans' groups;
- disbelieving in global warming and climate change;
- urging the reckless display and usage of nuclear weapons;
- belittling the U.S.'s status on the world stage;
- insulting Pope Francis;
- never really disavowing his "birther" claims about President Obama;
- disempowering America's democratic institutions by claiming they're "rigged."

So, in clear view of the positive aspects of Hillary Clinton's talents and experience, and because of the despicable facets of Donald Trump's character, behavior, and overall unfitness for the office, tomorrow I will gladly vote for Hillary Clinton as president.

It feels good to be clear and forthright with you all, and I thank you for your indulgence of this overly long missive. I pray you will vote your conscience tomorrow, and that you will rest in relative comfort in your choices.

Years from now, when conversations turn to the tone, the tenor, and the tempestuousness of this year's campaign, I hope you will find some comfort — maybe even encouragement — in the choice your Uncle Bob made, regardless of the actual election results.

I have strong hopes that Hillary Clinton will win the presidency, and I have confidence that she would be a good president. But none of us knows how the contest will come out. May you be at peace with your choices. I am at peace with mine.

All my love,
Uncle Bob

Inauguration Day — January 20, 2017

Dear Christopher, Matthew, Nicholas, Catherine, and Lincoln,

I'm writing to you all on matters similar to what I wrote on two-and-a-half months ago: about what our electoral system has wrought, and about the implications of the election of Donald Trump. Again, I want you to know where your uncle is positioned during this most unusual moment in history. My public roles in the ongoing endeavors of What U Can Do — in terms of voter registration, voter education, and citizenship involvement — continue to be obstacles to a full-throated, public declaration of my leanings regarding specific political candidates and parties. But I feel compelled to share with you personally some of my responses and reflections about what has transpired.

On the day that Donald Trump is sworn in as the 45th president of the United States, I still believe what I said in my previous letter about him being a "dastardly candidate for the Republicans, but also one of the most repugnant candidates in the history of American politics." I still believe he has acted in ways that are patently racist, deceitful, fact-averse, insulting, misogynistic, xenophobic, homophobic, belligerent, and bullying.

And yet ... he *is* our new President. I am not a member of the crowd that eschews any connection with Donald Trump, declaring he is "Not My President." He will indeed occupy that office, presumably for the next four years. What he says and does will have profound effects on us all and on the world. Therefore, in actual reality he is the president for all U.S. citizens, whether we like it or not. To say otherwise is to advocate and act for secession, like the Confederacy did 157 years ago.

Am I pleased by the fact that Trump is our 45th president? Absolutely not. Am I, by turns, embarrassed and occasionally ashamed that our nation has elected him? Yes. Do I wonder how in the world the citizens of the United States ever came to elect someone of Trump's ilk? Every day since the election!

By simply seeing the truth of Trump's ascendency to the post of "leader of the free world," I am not saying that one should do nothing in the face of what promises to be a long, bumpy ride.

For Democrats like me who were disappointed to the marrow of our bones by the results of our nation's collective political will on November 8 — and for others who are independent in their political leanings but who nonetheless were disgusted by Trumps' election — this is a time of testing, requiring vigilance, patience, hard work, and a healthy sense of humor.

For some people "resistance" will be the default position, and an abiding theme in their lives. In a nation as bitterly divided as ours is at this moment — with Hillary Clinton having received nearly 3 million more votes than Trump — we can't help but encounter resistance and protest over anything and everything President Trump will do.

But I believe vigilance may be the key to it all. Time will likely confirm that Trump is the president with the highest "Transactional Quotient" in the history of the office. It seems that all matters — political, financial, social, and relational — are basically "transactional" from Trump's perspective. That is, all things, all groups, all connections, all relationships are to be understood as transactions of a "deal" nature. Recall how Trump spoke *ad nauseum* on the campaign trail about making the "best deals." Deals, he kept reminding us, were the *sine qua non* of his presidential aspirations. And, nearly always, the deals he imagined had to do with material worth. Deals — this for that, tit for tat, quid pro quo — were (and now are) part of his "deal" with America.

But values like loyalty, trust, love, fidelity, truthfulness are not subject — finally and foundationally — to deal-making. (Are they really "values" any longer if they can be bought or sold or traded like one commodity among other commodities?) To live a truly ethical, soundly moral, and utmost human life, we are called to embody our values in our very essence, in our character, not trade them in for a better "deal."

Which leads to what might be the greatest worry, character. Trump is not an ideologue, unless "ideology" can include what appears as egomania, i.e., obsessive preoccupation with one's self. Since Trump is not wedded to a core set of abstract political, theological, or philosophical principles, then all we have to go on is his character, i.e., his supposed moral center, what he stands for, those values outside of himself to which he is committed. And his "character" is exceedingly hard to define. Some of us would quickly observe that "character" is always hard to discern in a narcissist. And I believe serious citizens would be hard-pressed to disagree with that assessment since an avalanche of evidence shows Trump's consistent focus on self-aggrandizement.

In the face of all these concerns, one could (and perhaps should) worry all the more about our country's future under Trump's leadership. Vigilance, again, is in order. I am convinced that if we citizens do our job and press our concerns on our elected officials and everyone with a listening ear in the administration, our democracy will not ultimately be in peril.

And while it is small comfort, there is some reassurance in knowing that we've had bad presidents, and presidents who have acted badly, before. A brief, representative list would surely include the following:

- Don't ask Native Americans to honor any monument celebrating Andrew Jackson, who authorized the "Trail of Tears" and its horrific displacement and cultural annihilation.

- Andrew Johnson, whose recklessness and alcoholism nearly undid some of Abraham Lincoln's noblest and most far-reaching accomplishments.

- James Buchanan, who endorsed the Dred Scott decision, one of the Supreme Court's most ignoble moments.

- Warren G. Harding, whose lackadaisical attitude let the U.S. Treasury be nearly plundered and who said of himself, "I am not fit for this office and should never have been here."

- Franklin Roosevelt's turning away of the transatlantic ocean liner *M.S. St. Louis*, full of Jewish immigrants seeking asylum from Nazi Germany in 1939, and his endorsement and signing of Executive Order 9066, mandating the imprisonment of some 120,000 U.S. citizens of Japanese ancestry in internment camps from 1942 until the end of the World War II in 1945.

- And, of course, Richard Nixon, whose paranoia and criminal actions in the shameful Watergate scandal led to the biggest constitutional crisis in modern U.S. history.

- Ronald Reagan, who radically multiplied the ranks of the homeless by defunding government programs (especially group homes) for the emotionally and psychological disabled.

- And how often we've been reminded this past year of Bill Clinton's sexual dalliances and his lying to the American people.

Oh, yes, we've elected bad presidents, and presidents who acted badly, before. But, because we've prevailed before, I believe we can prevail again.

So here I offer a baker's dozen of urgings for your consideration — as we behold the confirmation of various scandal-prone candidates for Cabinet positions (perhaps exceeding those of previous administrations), as we suffer through our new president's actions as Bloviator-in-Chief, as we wade through the morass of misdirection and propaganda, as we try to disentangle fact from fiction about Russia's tampering with the election — beginning today, and continuing hereafter:

- Let us register as many voters as we can, wherever we are, and let us promote voter registration, voter education, and citizenship involvement with and among as many folks as we can possibly meet.

- Let us press our concerns on our Congressional representatives and senators. (I intend to maintain close contact with Congressman Emanuel Cleaver II from Kansas City and Senators McCaskill and Blunt from Missouri.)

- Let us stand up for those who may lose their health care coverage — and possibly their lives — if there's a radical change, dilution, or dismantling of the Affordable Care Act.

- Let us join with others in the wider community to promote and advocate for the welfare and well-being of the poor, and especially for children.

- Let us champion diversity and inclusiveness for all people, and vociferously resist xenophobic intolerance of others because of racial, religious, national origin, gender-identity, sexual orientation, or any other differences. (This is truly the American way.)
- Let us support and defend immigrants and their children against deportation, slander, and dehumanization.
- Let us pray fervently and persistently for President Trump to be imbued with wisdom, courage, and humility in the daily exercise of his office.
- Let us hope for a transformation in our nation, away from the nationalistic tribalism that has conquered the day, and toward a vigorous embrace of the collective insight and religious pluralism that has been a hallmark of the United States at its best.
- Let us release the rancor in our spirits and move into a season of active waiting, watching, and striving for an America that works for all of us, and especially for those who have endured the long nightmare of poverty.
- Let us be vigilant against the demagoguery, bigotry, misinformation, and chaotic confusion sown by the likes of Steve Bannon and others who seek to undermine our trust in each other, our trust in our own sensibilities, our trust in a free press, and our trust in the progress made thus far beyond the abject racism, sexism, and divisiveness of previous eras.
- Let us be aware of the politics of improvisational contradiction apparently being used by Trump — and crafted by Steve Bannon? — whereby observations about Trump by the press and his critics are then used in Trump's own statements to describe those he opposes or views as enemies. Such tactics amount to propagandistic bullying.
- Let us remember that our *best* presidents have been the champions of others, the preservers of the dignity of all,

and genuine congratulators of the American people and not themselves.

- Let us love each other with fierce devotion and affection, and let us share that love with as many friends, colleagues, and others as we can.

I trust you all are well and will remain positive about the future. Some days, I think my generation has done a pathetically inadequate job of handing off to you a better world. (Fortunately, you all came along to help right the ship and make us all so much more faithful to the "better angels of our nature.") Remember: however dim or dark the prospects for a truly humane existence may now seem to some, and however dismal the views of those who condemn our condition today, there is always hope. And hope finally, always wins.

Love,
Uncle Bob

Independence Day — July 4, 2018

Dear Christopher, Matthew, Nicholas, Catherine, and Lincoln:

Greetings and Happy Fourth of July!

We are now into the 18th month of the current administration, and I want to convey my hopes, dreams, and concerns for our mutual future — the future of our nation and the world. I do so now without the constraints connected with my previous work with What U Can Do, the nonprofit voter empowerment endeavor which I served as Community Engagement Coordinator for nearly two years.

Perhaps like you, over the past two years, between the deep throes of the 2016 presidential campaign and this year's birthday celebrations for our nation, I've been thinking a lot about democracy. If the last two years have taught us anything about our national predicament it is this: Democracy is hard.

Democracy — the kind of democracy that we Americans say we participate in, the kind of democracy that is at the foundation of the U. S. experiment at its very best, the kind of democracy that countless patriots have believed they were fighting and dying for — is excruciatingly difficult to fulfill. Any leader who promotes an "easy" solution for the plethora of nettlesome problems within a democratic nation is only peddling snake oil, as they used to say. In other words, such a leader is a charlatan.

Democracy is hard because it is complicated. Democracy is hard because it involves compromise. Democracy is hard because it is suffused with competing visions and alternative approaches to nearly every issue engaged in public life.

Despite the difficulties of democracy, I am absolutely convinced it is still worth it. The old aphorism, while admittedly hackneyed, is still true: *Democracy is the worst form of government, except for all the others.*

Of course, the best form of democracy is based on the premier values within the human community. Chief among these values are honesty and truth-telling.

As history has shown again and again, those who wish to dissolve democratic ideals and establish dictatorial power will first attack journalists in particular and the truth in general. Fascists galore have practiced what Joseph Goebbels codified for

Nazi propaganda: *Tell a lie long enough and usually people will come to believe it.*

Honesty, like democracy, is difficult.

Honesty is difficult because it entails the limitations of human discourse. (To say one thing is to refrain from saying something else.) Even when rendered with absolute conviction and good faith, one's assertions can require restating, clarification, and reframing. Such discourse takes time, patience, and care, all of which are difficult to manage. When an elected official regularly unleashes a barrage of vitriolic attacks and inane assertions via Twitter or Facebook, patience and care are severely undercut. The "Twitterization" of our public discourse contributes mightily to what John Dewey once called "the cult of irrationality."

I've also been thinking about another key component of any functioning democracy, namely integrity.

Personal, communal, and national expressions of integrity — that is, meaning what you say and saying what you mean, acting on the basis of consistent morality, and coherently reflecting and expressing one's moral convictions — are essential for any democratic nation to achieve its highest goals, particularly the United States and our lofty ideals of "Life, Liberty, and the pursuit of Happiness."

Along with honesty and integrity, I can't help but think about respect as a key ingredient of democracy and its flourishing.

Respect is often reflected in our language, especially the language we use to describe others. Truly respectful leaders in our nation know that we are a vast stew of a nation, blessed by the rich reserves of diversity inherent among a rainbow array of U.S. citizens. Also, respectful leaders do not sully the reputations of other leaders with petty slighting or vulgar slandering. Leaders who are committed to respecting all persons would never use racist innuendo to attack any group of human beings — such leaders would not speak of immigrants as "infesting" our nation.

Along with honesty, integrity, and respect as key features of a strong democracy, I've been musing a lot about compassion.

Compassion is as crucial to democracy as justice is. Without compassion, a nation's government can deteriorate into reptilian brutality.

The quality of compassion, and the concomitant virtues of kindness and mercifulness, are the ultimate characteristics that determine the legacies by which our greatest leaders are remembered. No leader can authentically claim to love freedom who lacks compassion for those yearning for a more fulsome experience of freedom and freedom's gifts.

So, democracy and honesty, integrity, respect, and compassion — these are the things I've been thinking about, as I ponder where we are as a nation on the occasion of our national birthday party.

My ponderings have led me to an assessment shared by millions of folks: By almost every measure, we are in danger. And a focus on the seeming robustness of the economy cannot mask the trouble.

Many are beginning to discern that "the system" is rigged against them, and rigged by none other than those who occupy the highest offices in the land, as they accrue more advantage for themselves. Leaders whose focus is on more fame for their brands, more attention for their egos, and more money for their supposed empires are deleterious to democracy. Because of the tax bill, 86 million middle-class Americans will have their overall taxes raised, and 83% of the benefit will go to the top 1% in terms of income. It would not surprise me at all if, years hence, world leaders report in memoirs, interviews, and public recollections that they laughed, mostly in derision, sometimes with incredulity, at the chaotic, nonsensical antics the current administration has demonstrated. Many of them are likely to plaintively ask in retrospect, "What was going on with you Americans, why didn't you do something, how did you let this happen?"

Beyond the economics of our nation, the trouble is plain to see. And the most troubling aspects of our predicament have to do with the character, or lack thereof, in the current administration and the chaos, confusion, and consternation abounding in our society.

Leaders who are so insecure and needy that they create a cutthroat atmosphere among administrative staffers are not worth following.

Leaders who are so willfully ignorant that they refuse to learn what a careful reading of history would teach them are not worth following.

Leaders who are autocratic, dictatorial, and megalomaniacal in their leadership styles are not worth following.

Leaders who daily commit serial misrepresentations, blatant misdirection, and provably false declarations are not worth following.

Leaders who lack humility as a major tool in their toolbox are not worthy of support. (Every great American leader who has ever captured my attention – Abraham Lincoln, Frederick Douglass, Franklin D. Roosevelt, Martin Luther King, Jr., Fannie Lou Hamer, Sitting Bull, Marian Wright Edelman, Cesar Chavez, Barbara Jordan, and the list could go on and on – has expressed deep-seated humility in the face of life's and the world's incessant dilemmas regarding fairness, equity, living the good life, sharing heartache and setbacks with others, and the vicissitudes of human existence. How utterly vulgar, how nauseatingly offensive, and how egregiously indefensible is the promotion of one's achievements and one's supposed superiority over previous leaders as people gather at the White House for a National Day of Prayer.)

And leaders who authorize policies of maltreatment of children as being "necessary" for the supposed fulfillment of U.S. immigration laws are not worthy of endorsement. (The separation of young migrant children from their parents at U.S. borders is a form of child abuse and ruthless dehumanization.)

The executive branch of our government, along with the leadership in the U.S. House of Representatives and the U.S. Senate, have put the alternatives of our times in drastic relief:

- respectful mutuality vs. sycophantic loyalty
- the ability to clearly own one's mistakes vs. idiotic denials of making mistakes
- the strength of humility vs. the weakness of arrogance
- wise graciousness vs. brutal one-upmanship
- respect for the contributions of past leaders vs. denigration of all previous leaders

- deep appreciation of the free press vs. the disgraceful attack on the press as "enemy of the people"
- compassion vs. cruelty
- the joys of sharing common purpose vs. the bitterness of people being pitted against one another
- methodical diplomacy in a world endangered by nuclear weaponry and ecological destruction vs. reckless alliances with dictators and fascistic leaders

I don't know how we can completely disentangle ourselves from our current predicament, but I believe we must commit, at the very least, to the following actions:

- Become aware of and knowledgeable about local, state, federal, and global issues
- Get to know your local, state, and U.S. elected officials and their bed-rock commitments and stated policy views.
- Vote in every possible election.
- Encourage and remind our peers, friends, and colleagues to exercise their citizenship by voting in every possible election.
- Register more and more eligible voters, particularly among our nation's youth.
- Fight voter suppression and voter roll purging.
- Maintain a posture of hopefulness through prayer, reading, conversations with like-minded friends and family members, and sharing in the communities where you live.
- Stand up for the values of honesty, integrity, respect, and compassion as often as we can, in as many venues as we can, with as much energy and courage as we can.
- Trust that since our nation has weathered troubling predicaments before, we can do so once again.

Please know this beyond any doubting: I love you all and will do all I can to fashion a better world for you and your children and your children's children. Such love is the impetus for this letter.

All my love,
Uncle Bob

SUNDRIES

George Nakashima: "To go to sleep with an honest face."

A while back, on a sunlit afternoon, near an illuminating window within the confines of the Metropolitan Museum of Art, as a new graduate of divinity school I happened upon a small table by George Nakashima. Astounding in its simplicity, beautiful in form, shining in appearance, it was immediately apparent why that table had attained the status of art and been deemed worthy of exhibition.

One of Nakashima's hallmark achievements, I would learn later, is a Peace Table he made for the United Nations. It turns out he was also an insightful soul, chock-full of good counsel for life, as well as knowledge of wood and its wonders.

Nakashima mentored many wood artists, always encouraging them to do their work in such a way, with such integrity, that they could "go to sleep at night with an honest face."

Sterling advice for us all, indeed, whether or not we know much about wood.

The "Left Behind" Phenomenon

The popularity of LaHaye and Jenkins' *Left Behind* novels is but one expression of a long, persistent line of questioning pursued by the religious: How will human life end? What is the purpose and destination of our existence? The fear that attends such pondering has also been with the human family for a long time.

A generation ago, Hal Lindsey's *The Late Great Planet Earth* scared some folks into thinking that the year 2000 would witness the end of the world. Before Lindsey's radically loose interpretation of the Book of Revelation, upon which, he asserted, his novelistic book was based, there were other doomsayers who predicted the end of the world with absolute certainty.

At nearly every turn toward the option of war by the world's community of nations, gloom-and-doom purveyors have predicted the end of all things.

In the clutch of deadly diseases, particularly pandemic afflictions such as the plague of the Middle Ages, or in the midst of the global onslaught of HIV/AIDS, the human community quickly moves toward apocalyptic visions.

The specter of nuclear war once cast an end-times shadow over much of the American political scene and our relations with other nations. Many can recall how that shadow influenced the 1964 presidential election contest between President Lyndon Johnson and Senator Barry Goldwater.

All of which goes to show how saturated with apocalyptic talk and end-times thinking human history is — especially today, in a world "wired to the max" for instant communication and thus deluged with information.

The Book of Revelation is an expression of apocalyptic, end-times thinking, but it is also so much more. Written in the midst of the roiling troubles of the early Christians, its ultimate goal was to comfort those who were afflicted and oppressed. It has offered such consolation and encouragement to generations of faithful Christians since it was first circulated. The eschatology ("study of the last things") it contains may not make as much sense to 21st-century Christians as it did to our first-century brothers and sisters, but its message of hope and the power of enduring can and does resonate with us.

Any apocalyptic vision that would claim to be Christian, any eschatology that would be in harmony with the claims and callings of Jesus of Nazareth, will strike the clarion note of the Resurrection. For it is in the overcoming of all things by God's love-infused, life-affirming grace that we understand life's ultimate meaning.

Frederick Buechner put it best, I believe, when he defined the true essence of Christian faith: "The resurrection means that the worst thing is never the last thing." That's a word that all of us, including LaHaye and Jenkins, need to hear and heed.

Tales from the Trail

Brookside Trail, as we Brooksiders informally call it (instead of its official name, "The Harry Wiggins Trolley Track Trail"), is a grace-laced pathway to health, beauty, community bonding, and revelation.

Stretching from Volker and Brookside boulevards all the way to 85th Street and Prospect Avenue, it offers anyone who traverses its 6.5 miles plenty of opportunities to enhance their quality of life, and to meet new friends.

As it parallels Brookside Boulevard and/or Wornall Road and/or Main Street, it offers extraordinary vistas of nature and humanity.

Being a frequent walker, I appreciate the foresight of the Kansas City leaders who decided that the former trolley track-beds should be transformed into an urban trail for enjoyment by one and all.

I've learned and re-learned a lot on the trail.

- I've learned that etiquette is both important and inspiring. Saying "Good morning," "Morning," "Good afternoon," "Good evening," "Hello," or "Howdy" can be a day-changing encounter.
- I've discovered how bold robins can be once they've become accustomed to human creatures and once we human creatures leave the robins alone.
- I've experienced how a person can enjoy, exert, marvel, relax, ponder, and huff-and-puff one's way toward peace of mind in a mere 30 minutes.
- I've observed that there are more ways to walk and run and ride and mosey than you would ever imagine.
- I've noticed that there are more sizes and shapes of walkers, runners, riders, and moseyers than you would ever imagine.
- I've witnessed how revelation can come in the form of an earthworm or a cloudburst or an automobile manufacturer's logo, all on the same day.
- I've realized again how weather is an ever-changing phenomenon capable of surprising and dismaying those experiencing it in a minute's turning.

- I've learned that a trail can become an avenue of awareness, a pathway to keener perception, a portal to knowledge, an entrance into encounter, a way into wonder, and a track toward truth.

Snow on Snow on Snow

I'm beginning to see why the Central Alaskan Yupik language has at least a dozen different words for snow. Nearly that many kinds of the white stuff have descended on Kansas City since Christmas Eve.

- There's the thrilling powder that beckons sledders of all sizes, shapes, and ages to Brookside Park and other picturesque inclines.
- There's the electric snow that seems to stream upward within the beams of Community's Steeple of Light.
- There's the cashmere snow that's soft and downy, falling fast during the coldest temperatures, best encountered with cashmere-lined gloves.
- There's the sloppy mush that falls in dollops and sometimes melts right away. (When it doesn't melt, it's heavy to shovel but normally doesn't leave an icy trace.)
- There's the obstacle-course snow that results from snow removal crews piling up big drifts of the stuff in the middle of parking lots and shopping areas.
- There's desert-sands snow that scurries across the road, spraying everywhere when your vehicle passes through it.
- There's pellet snow that masquerades as sleet but accumulates in clumps of micro-fine cannonballs.
- There's furious snow that slants and stabs at your cheekbones, difficult to appreciate, almost impossible to look at, when you're scraping a windshield.
- There's filigree snow that comes, almost always before or after a major snowfall, and alights on windows in intricate patterns of lacy beauty.
- There's meditative snow, a.k.a. coffee-and-tea-time snow, that descends completely vertically, without a trace of wind, hour after hour, and is the surest to instill wonder and awe.

Christina Rossetti's wonderful poem, now a treasured song of the season, "In the Bleak Midwinter," has it just right for us these days: "Earth stood hard as iron, water like a stone; / Snow had fallen, snow on snow, snow on snow."

Sharing Joy (Instead of Happiness) with Friends

While he was contemplating the sheer variety and liveliness of creatures in nature, Thoreau would exclaim, "Surely joy is the condition of life." When we think of our friends, surely joy is the condition of life with them:

- The joy of a shared task and its fulfillment;
- The joy of celebrating another's achievements;
- The joy of overcoming a setback or a sorrow or an excruciating loss;
- The joy of sharing stirring worship together in harmonious, awe-inspiring ways.

Byron was right when he said, "All who joy would win / Must share it, — Happiness was born a twin." But let us also note that there are definite differences between happiness and joy.

Happiness is a full stomach and a checking account in the black and a favorite car.

Happiness is the absence of irritation and a lack of troubles and the promise of pleasant days in the on-going journey of a pleasant life.

Happiness is your hometown team having a winning record and getting all your ducks in a row and all the leaves raked and bagged and set on the curb.

Happiness is fleeting, though, and the least wind can blow happiness right into the wild blue yonder.

Joy, on the other hand, is a grandmother's embrace and the glad light of daybreak and a laugh shared with someone in the cancer treatment center.

Joy is a high "C" piercing into the upper reaches of a sanctuary (and right through the center of your soul) and the soldiers coming home safe and whole and able to begin life anew.

Joy nearly always implies two or more. It needs to be shared.

From the poorest of the poor to those who have no financial worries whatsoever, joy is shared among friends.

In fact, shared joy may be the holiest joy that can be experienced. It is in friendship that we know the truth of the psalmist: "Weeping may endure for a night, but joy cometh in the morning" (Ps. 30:5).

There is an old saying: "Some people bring joy wherever they go. Other people bring joy whenever they go."

Thank God for the gift of joyous friendships that bring us some of the sweetest and most gracious experiences we ever know.

Looking for a Sign

A young girl waited at the summit of the Smoky Mountains. Since four in the morning she had been hunkered down at the pinnacle of Mount LeConte, waiting for the sun to leap up over the edge of the horizon and blaze forth in all its glory. But the mountaintop sunrise didn't happen that way.

Instead, the ebony sky first turned a deep indigo, then navy blue, then purple, and then lighter and lighter until it was almost violet. She couldn't remember exactly when, but red appeared from somewhere, and then orange, and then something more and more like pure gold. And after a while it seemed that the sun just arrived, not as a fiery ball but as a familiar sentinel of light, as if it had been there all along.

Jesus cautioned that the kingdom of God will arrive silently and seemingly unseen, not bluntly or overtly. It will come when and where we don't expect it. In fact, Jesus declared, it's already coming in our hearts and minds and within the larger core of the community. ("The kingdom of God is not coming with signs to be observed ... for behold, the kingdom of God is in the midst of you." — Luke 17:20-21)

What are the signs you have been looking for during your own faith journey? How big would a sign have to be for you to be convinced that God's reign of love and justice is a tangible reality? As big as a billboard? Electrified, in neon?

Would an audible sound suffice, say, over a loudspeaker? Or would it be something you felt all of a sudden in the midst of a sensitive, quiet moment? Where is God's reign already in your midst?

Consider these questions and sharpen your faith by naming five instances, occasions, places, events, or people to which you can point as evidence of God's kingdom. I am sure that remembering such signs will lift the spirit and calm the fevered mind.

Musing About Museums

I'm quite fond of the quote that goes, "Churches are not museums for saints but hospitals for sinners." I resonate with the verity expressed in the adage, and, as my friends, acquaintances, and associates know, I am committed to the idea that all churches should be not just repositories for the past but rather vibrant, helping, healing, and hope-filled places for those struggling for a better life in all dimensions — spiritually, physically, emotionally, relationally, socially, civically, denominationally, nationally, and globally.

But lately I've discovered that adherence to such a time-honored quote is giving museums a bad name. Perhaps my thinking has been quickened by the exquisite Nelson-Atkins Museum of Art, and its addition of the Bloch building which thrills us with its extraordinary architecture. Perhaps it's the Kemper Contemporary Art Museum, whose inspirational exhibitions offer startling new ways of seeing the world and humanity's potential for growth and progress.

Maybe my change of heart about the metaphor of museums has to do with the real meaning of the word "museum" itself: "a building, place, or institution devoted to the acquisition, conservation, study, exhibition, and educational interpretation of objects having scientific, historical, or artistic value."

But the origins of "museum" point to a grander purpose. The ancient Greeks, relying on the stories of their mythology, built "museums" as shrines for the Muses, the nine daughters of Mnemosyne and Zeus, each of whom presided as a guiding spirit and source of inspiration over a different art or science.

Of course, I do not believe in these deities and their nine progeny. But the notion of "muse" and "muses" does ring a bell.

Any poet knows that the muse can come or go in an instant.

Architects and engineers speak of being inspired by certain muses.

Musicians of all kinds have fertile and fallow times with their muses, as inspiration visits and departs from them. (The word "music" derives from the Greek word *musike*, which means "the art of the Muses."

And we all are amused and bemused by presences and events that tickle our funny bones and our fancies.

So let us consider museums in a different light and with new ears and eyes. Perhaps it's best to say that a museum is a "home for songs," the songs that an artist has in herself, the song that a culture once sang and might sing again, the songs that are inspired, brought to life within a child or an adult viewing a painting, peering at a bottle of brains, looking at a glass-encased pine-tarred baseball bat, or walking through a collection of prehistoric artifacts. The "songs" in any museum are never really kept there, for all songs are meant for transmittal, for singing and hearing and for passing on to yet other singers to come.

Jury Duty

Say the words, and groans rise up around you. Say the words, and it's almost like swearing. For a host of reasons, all of them understandable, the words "jury duty" prompt a host of negative reactions. Jury duty is definitely a disruption in the normal routine. It compels one and all in the jury panel to come to grips with either grisly scenarios or soul-numbing minutiae or both. And the pay truly is a pittance.

For years I'd heard all about jury duty but never experienced it. While I'd been passed over, year after year, friends and loved ones endured repeated jury summons and participation in several county and federal jury panels and actual trials. Then, *voila!*, in the last couple of years, I was called three times to give a day of my time for the purposes of justice in Jackson County.

Much to my disappointment, in all three instances I was not chosen for actual jury responsibilities. They say that clergy are routinely rejected for several reasons: too merciful, too reasonable, too sensitive, too forgiving. Actually that's not a bad reputation to have. It just doesn't go toward securing a seat on a jury. But the experiences leading up to the eventual rejections offered several points of good news to report.

People — The people who make up the pool of humanity summoned to become part of the various jury panels (the groups from which the actual juries are chosen) are impressive. The phrase "jury of one's peers" is more heartening than I'd been led to imagine. Individuals from nearly all walks of life and every social situation are there. The thoughtfulness and sociableness expressed by the individuals in the groups of which I have been a part have been exemplary. (The medical sector was missing, but that seems expectable; I suspect most of us would prefer that doctors, nurses, assistants and technicians not be called away from life-crisis situations.)

Process — The process was not only respectful and thorough but also interesting. The men and women who guided the jury selection process were informative, witty, compassionate, and clear. The video about the parameters of jury duty kept our attention with helpful details described by local celebrities (news anchor Elizabeth Alex, baseball Hall-of-Famer George Brett, weatherman Brian Busby, news columnist

Charles Gusewelle) and judicial personnel. The notion of "voir dire" — telling the truth — by which the prosecution and defense counsels sought to discern the best possible candidates for the jury became a survey of the human dramas lived out by Jackson Countians.

Purpose — Beyond the bedrock foundation of the ideal American justice system — the presumption of innocence — is the overarching purpose of the jury process: to render justice in as fair and democratic a manner as possible. The people and process I beheld have given me greater confidence in the ultimate purpose of jury duty. Sure, there have been and, I assume, there will be, some miscarriages of justice and occasional cantankerous juries. In the best of circumstances, democracy is a flawed experiment in the affairs of the human community. But still, it remains the most preferable mode for governance and adjudicating disputes.

So now, apart from the privilege and elemental obligation to vote, no aspect of U.S. citizenship seems to me to be more precious than the task of jury duty. I heartily (and mindfully) recommend it.

Increasing Your "Up" Potential

1. Wake Up to the magnificent gifts and graces that are yours.
2. Let Up on moralizing about other people's behavior.
3. Loosen Up and be silly once in a while.
4. Lift Up your thanksgivings to God for who you are.
5. Give Up trying to do everything for everyone.
6. Stand Up for your faith and your perspectives on life.
7. Grow Up and move beyond your pretensions of being superior.
8. Face Up to what needs changing and change it.
9. Open Up to the love around and within you.
10. Dress Up however you want.

In the Midst of Winter

Recently, on one of the warmer afternoons granted to us during the latest cold spell, I encountered an epiphany while enjoying a leisurely walk along Brush Creek. In fact, it was nearly shirt-sleeve weather, with adequate sun to shine on all of the strollers, walkers, dog-lovers, and other winter wonderers on the sidewalks just south of the Plaza.

The epiphany came in the form of the creek's frozen surface, a glistening glaze of reflections, frost, and contorted shapes that had been trapped, not unlike mosquitoes in amber, just below the surface. There were beer bottles, wine bottles, a glove, someone's phone bill (lost intentionally or unintentionally?), magazines, shoes, a plastic duck, a program from a local theater, a gray glove, a red ball, sticks of all sizes, and numerous other items that would nearly blind you if your tried to see, really see, them all.

But most revealing of all were the cracks in the frozen surface. Cracks that were pencil-thin, cracks that were hairline-thin, cracks that ran jagged courses, and cracks that ran straight as a plumb line. Cracks that measured only centimeters long, and cracks that spanned the entire width of the creek. Millions and millions — or maybe even billions and billions, as Carl Sagan might have described them — of cracks, scurrying every which way.

I had never really paid much attention to the creek in winter, and maybe because it was a fresh scene for me, or maybe because of the sheer luminosity of the afternoon, there was something clearly to be learned from this epiphany.

The epiphany was quite straightforward and simple: *winter does not last forever, and Brush Creek has cracks to prove it.* Even "in the midst of winter," as Camus put it more poetically, I discovered there was within the scheme of things "an indomitable spring."

Even in the midst of the cold, there are signs of the cold's abating. Even in the midst of frozen winter, there were signs of the coming thaw. Even in the midst of circumstance where little life is shown and time seems to be at a standstill, life is driving toward warmth and growth and change. Even in the midst of that which is as still as stone and colder than anything imaginable, there is the promise of a melting of that which is frozen solid. Even in the midst of seeming suspended animation, there is a forecast of forthcoming movement. Even in the midst of that which is fixed, there are signs that flux will eventually have its day.

All of which gives me hope, especially during any new snowfalls and chilly temperatures. Despite the present frozen surfaces of what we encounter — literally and metaphorically — there are always good hopes provided by the cracks.

Let me know soon where the tundra is melting a bit, where the cracks are appearing for you, and let us share the hope.

Gratitude and Resolve at the Wall

On a sunlit Saturday in May, Kansas City's Liberty Memorial was blessed to host the presence of the Traveling Vietnam Memorial Wall, a 4/5 scale replica of the actual memorial in Washington, D.C.

Many people were there simply to pay their respects and to commemorate Memorial Day.

The wall's bare inscriptions of the names of the 58,303 Americans who died during the Vietnam War were a stark and painful reminder of the costs of war and the sacrifice given by loyal citizens and their families.

As was the case during my first trip to the actual memorial in our nation's capital, I experienced again at the Traveling Wall on Memorial Day a deep recognition of the impact of the Vietnam War on multiple generations of Americans and the need for healing and hope, most especially for our veterans and their families.

And, as with my first visit to the actual wall, so with this visit I saw my own name, right at the midway point of the wall, about shoulder high.

The name inscribed was actually "Robert M Hill," but the different middle initial did not blunt my shock.

Through a quick internet search, I came to discover that the "Robert Hill" on the wall was from Starkville, Mississippi, and that he died at the age of 24, at Pleiku, on November 15, 1965, almost three months to the day from when he began his tour of duty.

I also learned that his "Casualty Type" was "Hostile" and that he "died outright," meaning that whatever suffering he might have encountered was hopefully minimal.

Seeing my own face reflected back at me with my name on the wall, I realized, *we all face ourselves and our relationship to the war through those remembered there.*

And I knew, with a new and unrelenting urgency, that we all have an abiding stake in what happens to each and every person whom our nation ever sends into harm's way.

As I walked away from the Traveling Wall, I offered a silent prayer, a prayer that was, as the war was, complicated, full of poignant thanks for those who so willingly served, anguished grief over the collective blundering that resulted in so many deaths, and resolve to help, as best I can, those who remain and those still coming home from further wars.

Graciousness

If you had to bet your religious farm or wager your last spiritual coin or put all your theological eggs in one basket, grace would be more than an adequate choice.

Grace is the *sine qua non* of the Christian life.

It is the center of the gospel message of love and care for each and all of God's creatures.

When we examine the life of Jesus, grace and graciousness are both his identity and his destiny.

Whether we're at the beginning of a new year or at the tail end of an old one, whether we're experiencing times of plenty or a stretch of need, whether we're down on our luck or in high cotton, whether we're plentifully satisfied or desperately empty, whether we're feeling fine or we're totally grim — there is no time when we cannot express graciousness toward others.

Initiating graciousness toward others comes easily to some, harder to others. But the receiving of graciousness is appreciated by everybody.

Through the rest of this week consider daily the following questions:

(1) Because grace is both the grounding gravity and the loving levitation of my life, how can I share grace with those around me?

(2) Because I know how pleasurable it is to receive graciousness and how delightful it is to pass along graciousness to another, how will I increase the graciousness quotient in my daily walk with God and neighbors?

Dreaming

When was the last time you were enthused by one of your dreams? When did you last tell someone about a very special dream? Are your dreams shimmering, startling, breath-taking experiences, causing you to sit bolt upright and make an assessment of your life? Or are they lukewarm, lacking in that which would make them memorable?

Dreaming, as any physician and any tender grandparent will tell you, is absolutely essential for a sane and healthy life. In fact, dreaming is crucially necessary for a bountiful life.

To maintain proper physical health, we must secure the proper amount of REM sleep and the kind of slumber, whether distinctly remembered or not, that entails adequate unconscious dreaming. To make significant contributions in the world — at school, on the job, in their faith communities, as citizens, or in their families — people must maintain and nourish a healthy stock of conscious dreams which guide their courses and inspire their achievements.

Dreaming is what the World Series is about.

Dreaming is what Martin Luther King was about.

Dreaming is what Olympic hopefuls do as they anticipate their competition.

Dreaming is what parents do as they gaze upon the faces of their children and consider the horizon of their children's future.

Dreaming is what a retiree does as she yearns to find a place of service where she can be of use in the ripeness of her maturity.

Dreaming is what engaged couples do as they plan for their wedding celebrations.

Dreaming is the order of the day in every physical therapy room in every hospital in the world.

Dreaming is the focus of first-graders on the first day of school and parents-to-be in the adoption agency waiting room and Sunday School teachers on Saturday nights and Sunday mornings and cancer researchers every day.

Dreaming is the prescribed dietary supplement for athletes and GED recipients and city planners and civil rights activists and seminary students.

For any developing human being, dreaming is as necessary as oxygen.

For any advancing culture, dreaming is as irreplaceable as the sun.

For artists before a canvas, writers at their desks, and clergy behind their pulpits, one's life-work is to dreaming as walking is to gravity: you can't do one without the other.

Coming Home

"Home." Four little letters in one little English word, and yet connotations cascade over us as we try to tell what that word means. Some folks, after the attitude of Robert Frost, would sardonically declare that home is "the place where, when you go there, they have to take you in." For many, home is the "sweetest" locale.

For others it is that comforting feeling you get when you park your car in the driveway at the end of a long drive. Say it softly and sense how you feel: "Home."

For still others it's the way the front of the house looks, framed as it is by the sway of trees in agreeable response to a soft, late summer breeze. Home.

For returning college students it can be the sight of a clock tower or the front door of the library or the stretch of grass that swoops up to your dormitory. Home.

For the motorcyclist it can be the undulating ribbon of highway that seems to go on forever beneath clear blue skies. Home.

For the avid reader it can be how a brand-new book, just released by a favorite author, feels in the hands. Home.

For a three-year old it can be the smell of mother and the touch of father and the sight of a sibling and the smell of breakfast. Home.

For the life-long resident — regardless of the weather, despite any downturn in the local economy, no matter the growth or decline in population — it is superior to any other place on earth. Home.

For newlyweds it is a new locale of adventure and strangeness and a communion unlike any other one has ever experienced with any other human being ever. Home.

For the writer it is the sacred table and the appointed hour and the look out the window and the ritual dozing of the dog by the door. Home.

For the baseball player it is the familiar locker and the view from the dugout and the brilliance of the plate after the end of a home-run trot. Home.

For the politician it is the sight of the city limit sign and a familiar strip of businesses whose support is incalculable and the taste of her favorite cornbread in her favorite restaurant and the shout of "Hey, have I got a proposition for you" by constituents.

"Coming Home," when related to the Church, also has other connotations.

Members are enthused to speak of their "church home."

Countless folks throughout countless congregations in countless cities, towns, and villages have uttered nearly identical sentiments: "I'm so glad we found this church! When we came here, it just felt like we had come home."

Ultimately, "coming home" is what faith is all about. "Coming home" to a belief system that makes sense and fuels our lives with purpose and direction. "Coming home" to an intriguing and interesting band of brothers and sisters in the faith whose religious pilgrimage has an obvious integrity and a developing creativity. "Coming home" to a spiritual adventure where new light from previously unsuspected sources provides surprising insights and renewal of one's heart and mind. "Coming home" to ennobling traditions and challenging new ways of looking at one's set of tasks as a human being. "Coming home" to a way of celebrating the goodness and grace of God that you always believed was possible but had not seen demonstrated very often. "Coming home" to a new way of viewing the Bible and its relevance for today. "Coming home" to a comfortable and growing relationship with God and neighbor and self.

My hopes and prayers are fervent and consistent: may we all "come home" to God and to faith with a resounding sense of appreciation and excitement, knowing that your congregation is that place where, when you go there, they *want* to take you in — with contagious joy, loving warmth, and sincere welcome.

Autumn's Raiment

For at least two weeks every autumn, an explosion of color blankets Kansas City and the whole of Missouri and Kansas. The traditional eruption of color in the Northeast has usually already begun, though it may be late depending on rainfall and summer conditions. Low-lying locales in Arizona and Nevada and balmy settings like the coastal areas of Texas and Florida afford other graces but not so much the enrapturing "turning of the leaves" that we enjoy here.

As autumn's raiment is fully revealed, I suggest you make your way down Wornall Road and behold the colonnade of trees along the Harry Wiggins Trolley Track Trail (a.k.a. Brookside Trail) between Meyer and Gregory boulevards. Some afternoons, manifestations of God's grandeur, like a 21st century burning bush, will be blindingly present there. On some mornings, the glint of sunrise will caress the tree-tops there in mauve-and-magenta majesty and all creation will seem to have risen in praise.

Our regular lives, necessarily focused on the daily routine, may keep us from visiting picture-perfect displays of autumn's beauty in famous places elsewhere. But no worries, the beauty is already here, where you and I live, in our own famous places, right down the block and in your yard and here in the heart of the heart of the country on a stretch of neighborhood that waits to bless with effusive visual epiphanies.

There are many signs of God's gracings in the world, but few as arresting as Kansas City's oaks and maples offering up their generous evidence of holy transformation.

Letter to Catherine

Last week, my sister Becky gave birth to her third child and her first daughter, Catherine Elizabeth. Becky and her wonderful husband, Rick, along with their two sons, Christopher and Nicolas, welcomed this fragile new life with gladness and thanks, and with a sort of exhausted awe. Nestled in their home in Virginia near the magnificent Blue Parkway, they now take up their lives within the warm glow of a loving family and with warm communications from a doting uncle and gift-giving aunt.

In a time of war, a good, holy thing has happened. In the midst of our national preoccupation with the war, I began some musings which I wanted to communicate to Catherine so that she might know the style and the substance of the times into which she was born. Thus this missive which Becky and Rick will save for Catherine for later perusal.

Dear Catherine,

The year you were born will go down as the year when a great conflagration erupted in a portion of the world which has already experienced a seemingly endless series of wars and has known nearly ceaseless hate. In your birth and in the births of other precious babies like you lies the real hope of the world. We seem to be given a fresh chance at setting life aright whenever we are granted the priceless gift of new life such as yours.

We adults have not done a very good job of dealing with international disagreements. May we be forgiven for the legacy of our missed opportunities and mangled management of national frictions and regional differences.

Each and every day, the world becomes smaller. But Norman Cousins, who died the year before you were born, was right when he said, "Our problems are exacerbated by the fact that the world has become one before it has become whole."

The earth will be your friend if you will be friendly toward it. We are in a lot of trouble right now. In relation to the earth's health, the word is "urgency." We will urgently seek to remedy the mess we've made, but there will probably be challenge enough left for you to do a significant part in cleaning up the world when your turn comes around.

International relations and national politics and even community affairs, I suspect, begin with family relations. So, be a peacemaker with your brothers, the best way you know how. Always be kind and generous and honest and caring toward your parents. And always remember that you are loved by God, who also loves all other children wherever they are born.

Be yourself, as much as you can, and as much as it takes to be free and loving and full of God's graces which are yours for the taking. And as you go, your family will celebrate with you.

Know that you can always visit the home of your aunt and uncle as much as you want, especially during baseball season.

Love,
Uncle Bob

In Response to the Tragedy at Virginia Tech

The tragic killings that ravaged the Virginia Tech community in Blacksburg, Virginia, this past Monday morning, April 16, have broken all our hearts. A crazed gunman randomly slew students and teachers in a bizarre paroxysm of hate, confusion, and shadowy impulse. By Monday evening the calamity that had unfolded shocked our nation's psyche and bruised our collective soul. That we live in perilous times goes without saying. But the shock we're feeling now and our sense of brokenness still cause excruciating pain. In this incident of school-related gun violence, there is the terrible sense of a tragic return as we recall previous tragedies: Austin, Texas; Pearl, Mississippi; West Paducah, Kentucky; Springfield, Oregon; Jonesboro, Arkansas; Littleton, Colorado. Now, in response to the sorrow, we seek to find our way forward. As we proceed beyond the sadness of this week, I offer the following guiding suggestions:

> **(1) Pray.** Pray for the families of the victims, that they will receive comfort, care, and the solace of treasured memories and cherished relationships. Pray for the entire collegial community at Virginia Tech, that they will eventually move through this valley of the shadow of death with purpose and new insights about life's meaning and its precious nature. Pray for the citizens of Blacksburg, that they will feel the support of those outside their city limits who care deeply. Pray for the mercy-providing caregivers in congregations throughout the Blacksburg area, that they themselves will somehow know God's mercy in the midst of their endeavors.
>
> **(2) Grieve.** Many tears have been shed since news of the tragedy broke. And, on this national day of mourning, countless more tears will yet be cried. Mourning is always more than a ritualistic enactment. Our tears are sure signs of our humanity. And like God, in whose image we are created, our tears signal the sacred compassion that potentially lies at the foundation of every personality. So weep, cry, grieve. If you have

difficulty making sense of the tragedy, or you need of a shoulder to cry on or a listening ear in the midst of your grief, please feel free to call the church office and come and see any of the ministerial staff. Don't hesitate to call on us even if your need arises after this week. Each of us processes grief at a different pace and according to different rhythms.

(3) **Share Fellowship with Others.** Nearly every tragedy of conscious premeditation is born of desperate isolation. In response to the killings at Virginia Tech, it has been heartening to witness the annealing sense of togetherness and mutual concern being shared by a community intent on not letting violence have the last word. Alongside the inspiring "Hokies" at Virginia Tech, and with the people of Blacksburg, indeed all of Virginia, we are in this together. We struggle with this current strife not as ones who have no hope. And our hopefulness is found in the midst of fellowship shared in communities of care.

(4) **Revulsion and Anger are Natural.** Inevitably and naturally, revulsion at the events of this past Monday and expressions of anger at the perpetrator have occurred and will occur. We need not fear these emotions. Anger is a natural and healthy emotional response to a violated value. But staying stuck in a morass of anger is not healthy. So be angry, yes, but begin to transform your anger, through reflection and resolve, into a commitment to show compassion to victims, to change the world where you are, and to join with others in new actions. The tears wrought from anger and revulsion can be transformative forces in maximizing the possibilities of preventing similar such tragedies in the future.

(5) **Make a New Friend in the Congregation.** The ultimate blossoms of a community are found in the friendships that develop there. So let us cultivate communities where friendships flourish. Religious communities can

be the site of some of your most beautiful and caring friendships. Some of the deepest, most abiding relationships that you can experience happen in congregations. It is in a congregation where differences can be respected and honored. It is in congregations where individual talents can be appreciated and celebrated. Cliques never fare very well in congregations. Because we are an Easter people, there is the possibility of connections, community, and friendships for each one of us, no matter our status or condition in life. So I invite you to grow a new friend in the congregation, and see how your life will flourish.

From Agony to Agon: Responding to Charleston

Once more our nation is touched by excruciating agony. Once more we behold senseless killings founded upon willful ignorance and vengeful hatred bred by racism. Once more we cry out in agonizing despair, "How long, O Lord, how long?!"

In the midst of our shared agony over the situation in Charleston, South Carolina, where nine persons were murdered in the middle of a Bible study session at Emanuel African Methodist Episcopal Church on Wednesday night by a deranged domestic terrorist, I'm remembering three things.

The first is that the root of our English word "agony" is the Greek *αγον* (agon), meaning "struggle" or "contest." Our collective, agonizing pain in the face of this horrendous tragedy will eventually diminish from the place of prevalence it occupies now in our hearts and minds. But I pray that our engagement in the crucial struggle against racism and its evil effects will be enlarged and strengthened.

The second thing I'm remembering (and seeking to honor) is the list of names of those who died this past Wednesday night at Emanuel AME Church:

- Rev. Clementa Pinckney, the congregation's senior pastor
- Rev. Depayne Middleton Doctor
- Cynthia Hurd
- Susie Jackson
- Ethel Lance
- Tywanza Sanders
- Rev. Daniel Simmons
- Rev. Sharonda Coleman-Singleton
- Myra Thompson

I'm remembering these particular lives, these specific names, because in their incarnational reality a broader, deeper story is told. One was a mother of four children. One was a recent college graduate. One was in her eighties. Two were in their seventies. Four were clergy. All were precious children of God whose legacies and memories now beg for our response.

The third thing I'm remembering is the compelling answer Dorothy Soelle, a theologian of the first rank, once gave to a question about how we can understand evil when it happens in our midst. She said that in addition to asking why horrendous things happen, it's equally important to query, "What is this tragedy leading to?"

What are the deaths at Charleston leading to, as we move — not merely on, but forward into the future? Will the racist slayings in Charleston lead to the "race war" which Dylann Storm Roof apparently hoped to launch? Surely all of us hope not. Will the murderous havoc that brutalized the people of Emanuel leave us numb and paralyzed by an all-too-familiar hopelessness? Let us not yield to such a temptation.

Or will we transform agony into *agon*, a true struggle. Struggle means that we are called to do something, to take action to ameliorate and heal the hurting, broken places in our community and in our country. Struggle means that "it" — the problem of racism, the all-too-easy access to weapons of murderous destruction, or the daily desire of some to dominate over others — is *our* challenge, not a challenge for someone else. Our challenge. Our struggle. Our contest.

Let us recognize this moment not only for what it is but for what it can lead to, as we affirm that the last word about the Charleston tragedy is not simply the shared mourning which people of good will can and should express all across this country, but rather a call to act for goodness' sake, to *embody* our good will for all people.

The streets of heaven are too crowded today. Nine lives have been lost because of the insanity of hatred. Nine lives beseeching our renewed commitment to a struggle that is worthy.

The streets of heaven are too crowded today. Nine lives yearn for us to know what they know with holy clarity: God mourns with us in the midst of heartache and yet yearns for us to know we are loved and graced. God will wrestle with us in a holy *agon* and will never give up on us.

Knowing that God never gives up on us, how can we ever give up on God or the better angels of our nature? Knowing that

God never gives up on us, how can we ever give up on God's love and the hope, as Dr. King expressed it so well, that "darkness cannot drive out darkness, only light can; hatred can never conquer hate, only love can do that"? I and countless others, I am certain, with God's help, don't intend to give up.

A Statement of Commendation for "The Road to Maus" Exhibition (Sponsored by the Museum Without Walls)

UMKC Gallery of Art, University of Missouri-Kansas City
Nov. 3, 1994

These words are meant as commendations — commendations to the leaders and the forces of art which have brought *Maus* to this place. Our commendations abound for:

EDUCATORS

- Educators here in Kansas City, at the university level, and in high schools, middle schools, and elementary schools throughout the greater metropolis.

- Educators in religious institutions who will now call this gallery their *Shul*, their Sunday School, their Hebrew School, their mosque school.

CLERGY

- Clergy are also to be commended for being here, to learn once more an ancient lesson — that evil must always be vigilantly resisted.

ARTISTIC COMMUNITY

- Artists and their patrons are to be commended, possibly above all others, for daring to bring this amazing exhibit to Kansas City and for some of their admirable, ulterior motives — to startle but not to stun, to energize but not necessarily to electrify, to inspire but not to sensationalize that most daunting of questions for the 20th century — the question of human evil.

But most of all, we are to commend Art Spiegelman. Spiegelman has given us a wise and brilliant gift.

Now, Spiegelman proffers his gift within a context.

An artist like Spiegelman always has progenitors, those who bequeath a legacy and a heritage. And in his cartooning, Spiegelman is surely a modern-day inheritor of the ancient legacy of cartography, the essential art of mapping and charting.

Spiegelman the cartoonist, the cartographer, has given us a new map to the human soul and a chart for the human predicament.

If the *Kristallnacht* of 1938 — whose 56th anniversary, we should note, will be observed next Wednesday, Nov. 9 — was the beginning of Hitler's draconian and hellish "Final Solution," then Spiegelman's *Maus* is the commencement, during the last quarter of this century, of the "Initial Re-solution" of that hatred and enmity which one human being can promulgate upon another.

In these cartoons, Spiegelman has offered us not merely preparatory sketches for some other, grander artistic endeavor; neither has he given us comic strips, nor caricatures, nor drawings intended as sheer pieces of satire.

No, rather, Spiegelman joins his artistic impetus to that of Mauldin, Thurber, Herblock, Larson, Conrad, and, perhaps, in his more serious moments, Gary Trudeau, all of them great cartoon artists in their own right and after their own fashion.

But Spiegelman joins himself to others as well:

- To the cave dwellers in France who scrawled the primal outlines of their primitive world;
- To the adolescent students who have no other creative outlet but to tell their crude, comic-book stories, tentatively and genuinely, painfully and dreamily, on the inside covers of their textbooks;
- To the child whose finger-painted, penciled, crayoned, magic-markered, scribbled drawings are memorialized on refrigerator doors all over the world.

In short, these cartoons which we are privileged to view here draw upon the elemental impulse within the artistic quintessence of the human spirit. And that quintessence? It is truth, plain and simple truth.

Behold, then, on this good evening, these strong truths!

- The truth we see in the concentration camp numbers — 1-7-5-1-1-3 — which Spiegelman renders in careful, subtle detail in the arm of his father, Vladek, flailing on his exercise bike.

- The truth we see in the porcine snarl of the "kapo" in the exhibit piece entitled "Kapo's Revenge."

- The truth we see in the dripping-red pronouncement of the title lettering, "MAUS."

- The truth we see in the alarming photographic images of inmates from Auschwitz and Ravensbrück juxtaposed with the massed group of cartoon figures all dressed in *their* prison camp garb.

And in such a juxtaposition we behold a truth which we are all challenged to keep faith with, the shining truth never to be forgotten or glossed over or shuttled to the attics of our minds, an absolute truth: that no human being should ever become merely object, that no human endeavor should ever be subjected to "thingification."

Gaze upon the pictures of the actual inmates and they are all too famous. "Oh, yes, I've seen those," some might say with understandable melancholy. Perhaps some smart-alecks would feel (even if they did not express it), "Oh, yeah ... been there, done that ... so what ... another drab picture of that holocaust thing."

But then gaze upon Spiegelman's cartoon characters, and notice the revolting jolt in your stomach, the crack in your heart, the fibrillation in your soul, and perhaps, you will subsequently say, "Oh, no! That shouldn't be! What horror! What horror!"

And yes, that's exactly the point, isn't it?

Such horror should not happen to any *maus* — nor to any human.

Spiegelman thus helps to revivify the horror of the holocaust. And for this he is to be commended.

May this exhibit, attended by all of us who are to be commended for being here, help us to learn a wondrously simple, yet daringly beautiful lesson — *not to play any more heinous cat-and-mouse games upon the earth.*

"With hope and support, democracy will prevail."

(This open letter ran as an "As I See It" commentary in the *Kansas City Star*, on November 15, 2000, when I was serving as senior minister of Community Christian Church, Kansas City, Missouri.)

To the next President of the United States:

Despite the current uncertainty of the election, I join a host of citizens in the desire that the Florida recounts will be resolved with full fairness and justice and that we will proceed expeditiously toward a determination of the outcome.

As always, we will then live out democracy's shining ideals with tenacity and hope. And, as we have done in previous elections, we will gather together as one people and strive to unite our political will in support of our one nation.

We stand at an auspicious crossroads.

We are at once primed for a release from the cynicism and skepticism of the last decade and anxious about the possibilities for what Abraham Lincoln called "a new birth of freedom" in the next.

As you prepare to take office in January, please remember the concerns that citizens have expressed. While we do not and perhaps cannot ever share a unilateral vision for our nation's future, we all possess fervent passions for abiding ideals.

As you deliberate over the implementation of your agenda, please ponder these yearnings as well:

- *Campaign finance reform.* Please be a president of courage and foresight and do all you can for substantial reform in the ways we finance U.S. elections. Unless something of striking significance is done, vast campaign expenditures, particularly by corporate interests, will continue to shackle our nation in chains of greed. The miscreant costs of this year's elections have been perceived by many as a political obscenity of gross proportions. If nothing is done to reform campaign financing, the costs will be even greater than we can imagine.

- *Health care and education for all our children.* Surely we owe it to them to secure their physical well-being in all ways, especially through full-fledged health care, and to maximize their potential for life success through proper education. We will bankrupt their future with anything less.

- *Security for our senior citizens.* And surely we owe it to our elders to secure their hearts and minds from fear about the future. Those who have brought us thus far — through crucibles of crisis, sacrifice and unparalleled change — should receive our utmost respect and deepest thanks in the form of guaranteed proper care. We squander their future at the peril of our nation's soul.

- *A celebration of our country's diversity.* Throughout the presidential campaign and now in the throes of the tense process in Florida, we have beheld our nation's great diversity. As Americans, we are not simply special-interest groups. Instead, we are a magnificent quilt of humanity. But the quilt is in need of mending. As our president, you can help mend us so that we might be of one whole fabric.

As our president, you are no longer merely a leader of one party but of one nation. And you can do so very much to make us more truly one.

May the art of compromise in the pursuit of our common good be a ready implement in your political toolbox. And may your vision of our shared destiny be unclouded as to the gifts and graces of all.

This Sunday we will gather to celebrate Community Christian Church's annual "Thanksgiving Sunday."

We will celebrate the plentitude that is ours solely because of God's immeasurable generosity.

We are blessed as a congregation with a symphony of different tongues, representing a resplendent panorama of cultural heritages in our membership. You will be in our prayers, and we hope and trust you will keep us in yours.

LESSONS LEARNED

Kidney Stones: Tough and Deep-Truth Teachers

As many know, I've had a run-in over the past week and a half with a tough and deep-truth teacher.

Allow me to say how grateful I am for your tender mercies during a surprising and unwelcome bout with kidney stones.

The recent silence from these quarters occasioned by this run-in was compounded by the transition we've recently experienced because of some new computer equipment. This is why it may seem that I faded off the map recently, as far as e-mail communications go.

In the past ten days, I've gained an insider's view of some hospitals, after three visits to three different emergency rooms in three different states. I've come to appreciate the blessings of X-rays and CAT scans, the wondrous ways of pain medications, the exceeding grace a great urologist can be, and the comforting encouragement of countless friends through their prayers and expressions of concern.

Please know that your many kindnesses have been like manna.

I'm especially grateful for the care of Community's staff, particularly Rev. Dara Cobb (who ably stepped in for me in the pulpit on April 30), Donna Muiller, and also, of course, the members of Community's prayer chain team.

To Jimmy and Ken Mohler and J.D. and Jeanne Cooper, how can I ever thank you enough for your TLC at home?

And to Ken Mohler and Jerry and Donna Porter, thanks too, for being emissaries of mercy with the grace of the communion you shared around our kitchen table.

All of these experiences have deepened my appreciation of Community's family of faith and heightened my awareness of what a great privilege and mercy it is to be part of a caring congregation.

Kidney stones are tough and deep-truth teachers.

As you can imagine, I've had some time to reflect on 13 lessons it has brought into sharp focus.

1. We are all eventually dependent on the kindness of

others, sometimes strangers, when we are in extremis.

2. In an emergency room, there's almost always someone, usually just down the hall, who's in worse shape than you are.

3. It's hard to describe unrelenting pain in the middle of the night. And there's nothing quite like the euphoria of its ceasing.

4. More often than we may care to admit, sometimes all one can do in a medical crisis is wait. The trick is to do so with hope and a positive regard for everyone you meet.

5. There's humor in everything, especially if you're wearing one of those back-draft hospital gowns.

6. There's no personal indignity that's worth much worry when you're in the middle of a medical procedure.

7. Doctors and nurses are healers in ways they may never realize.

8. Words of authentic cheer, reassurance, and encouragement — but never glibness or flippancy — are absolutely wonderful to hear from nurses, doctors, and hospital volunteers.

9. Diet Sprite and saltine crackers can become communion.

10. Clear information and a thoroughly expressed diagnosis are beautiful salves for one's mind and spirit. They can have curative powers equal to medications and treatment protocols.

11. There's a rich texture of life in the backgrounds and histories of medical personnel. Even in medical emergency situations, there are opportunities for profound human encounter.

12. Illness can be like a spiritual discipline, if one takes advantage of the profound calm and eloquent silence it affords. Like a prayer vigil, lying on a gurney may be one of the most intimate times one can ever spend with God.

13. There is a great gulf between the levels of care one receives in a various hospitals. Our overall American health care system is not an equal-opportunity provider. Let the overhaul begin.

19 Things I Learned in New Orleans

"Let brotherly love continue. Do not neglect to show hospitality to strangers, for thereby some have entertained angels unawares." — Hebrews 13:1-2

The fourteen participants in Community's New Orleans Mission Trip have returned and, as promised, we've come back with stories aplenty. Our thanks are many. On the way to and from New Orleans we enjoyed the warm welcome of Rev. David Brice and Rev. Barbara Driscoll, who opened their hearts and the doors to the Family Life Center at Kings Highway Christian Church, Shreveport, Louisiana, for road-trip overnight stays. In Metairie, Rev. David Coleman and the kind members of First Christian Church of Greater New Orleans provided generous hospitality and gracious accommodations in their Family Life Center. We thank Rev. Josh Baird, coordinator for the Disciples' Gulf Coast mission stations in the area, sponsored by Disciples Home Missions and funded by the generosity of Week of Compassion, who guided us all along the way. We say thanks as well to the field representatives of the National Council of Churches, who included us in the Ecumenical Work Week they sponsored while we were there. And last, but never least, the prayers offered by Community's family of faith were truly strong sources of encouragement and support.

During our week in the Big Easy, our group worked on a total of five houses. Because of the hard-working character of Community's mission-trippers, there were occasions for some Community folks to be sent to multiple sites in the Seventh and Eighth Wards of New Orleans for jobs such as window framing, carpentry, mold remediation, termite fumigation, and gutting/tear-out. But the bulk of our work was done at the home of Ingrid Hearns at 2127 Tonti in New Orleans' Seventh Ward. Until Katrina came, Ingrid, a life-long resident of New Orleans, had lived in her traditional New Orleans "shot-gun" home with her brother Kerry and her dog Fred, an aging and lovable Rottweiler. A year after evacuating to South Carolina, Kerry died of cancer. Just this past April, Ingrid was allowed to return to her property and live in a FEMA trailer behind her home while restoration work proceeded. A teacher who served the New Orleans School System for 34 years prior to Hurricane Katrina,

Ingrid is now retired. Perhaps the best way to describe what was actually done at Ingrid's home is to quote (with permission) from a message she sent out to friends after our group had been on the job for three days:

> Once again I am overwhelmed by the generosity, love, and tireless labor of volunteers! This week, a group from Kansas City, Missouri, worked on my home and were joined today by a group from N.Y. Let me tell you what they accomplished toward restoration of my home ... They replaced bad weather boards up near the roof, they painted the house — 2 coats, they scraped and painted all downspouts, and ironwork, replaced bad studs in the bathroom and the hall ... replaced bad beams and sill under the kitchen and replaced a portion of the kitchen floor, took the windows out and scraped them, etc. ... They replaced the back door frame and my back door as well. I have a metal door now with a dead bolt! God has truly blessed me beyond my wildest dreams! When I returned I felt forgotten, beaten down, hopeless, faith shaken and thrown away. I had NO idea of where to begin or how! I was overwhelmed and ready to just give up and walk away from the only home I have known since birth ... All I saw was a Herculean task and knew that my funds were limited ... The volunteers are just so wonderful! No, they are phenomenal! What a blessing they have been in so many ways! ... I wish that Kerry was alive to see the way our home has been restored thus far. The house looks like it did when Kerry last painted it in 2002! It makes my heart feel so full! I am so wonderfully blessed! God IS still speaking!

And now for the "19 Things I Learned in New Orleans":

1. Handi-wipes can take off nearly any paint!
2. A tired body is a gift from God in preparation for a solid night of sleep.
3. If given the "up-and-at-'em" and "out-the-door" times, Community's faithful can rally and be on the bus at the break of dawn.
4. A pile of junk can be a sign of hope.
5. The pump stations and levee systems of New Orleans are nothing like anything I've ever experienced living in a city.

6. People are coming back to their neighborhoods pretty much in relation to the number of their neighbors who are coming back.
7. A neighborhood can come back, if given enough encouraging hope from local folks and friends from across the nation.
8. The talents among Community's faithful are untold and multitudinous.
9. You can't drink enough water when you're working outside in August in New Orleans.
10. What Oscar Romero declared, we all experienced: "Everyone can do something" – from painting to cooking to crafting woodwork to refinishing wrought-iron grill-work to driving the bus to shotgunning in the front seat to loading the bus to praying to assuming a positive attitude to tearing out to ...
11. There's really nothing like eating gumbo in the Crescent City.
12. It is people of faith and other non-profit groups who will see New Orleans and Gulfport and Slidell and Houma and Port Arthur and all other devastated locales to their eventual restoration.
13. The right kind of tools and the right size of paint brushes are true blessings. A cordless drill is one of the most ingenious creations of humanity.
14. Bitter experiences of injustice, unfairness, and desolation are made bearable and sometimes even sweet by the arrival of strangers at your door, or so Ingrid Hearns has said.
15. Lumber can be recycled like you've never imagined. Scavenging and cannibalizing among the houses of New Orleans for restoration projects must make for significant cost-savings in the overall restoration work in the Gulf Coast.
16. After a while, denominational, theological, and ecclesial distinctions fade into insignificance when you're trying

to get two coats of paint on the exterior of a house before keeling over because of the heat. Painting can be a true revelation of God's incarnational presence and an effective stimulus for ecumenical unity.

17. Lowe's and Home Depot are definitely good stock suggestions for the next five years in the Gulf Coast.

18. New Orleans will eventually gain a fresh emphasis on the first portion of its name. There will definitely be something "new" about New Orleans when it welcomes a full complement of its citizens, some homegrown and some new immigrants, into its embrace.

19. It's a toss-up as to who received more — the mission trip workers, who worked for three and a half days at 2127 Tonti in the Seventh Ward of New Orleans, or Ingrid Hearns, whose house is being restored there.

Seven Mandates for Marriage

I. **You shall have no other human loves before your spouse.** (Even within the growing number of blended families, the crucial relationship for strengthening and supporting the newly created household is the one between spouses.)

II. **You shall live without illusions concerning your mate.** (Loving each other realistically is a challenge and a delight, with plenty of occasions for exciting personal growth and forgiving support.)

III. **You shall not take each other for granted.** (To focus solely upon one's own needs and to neglect the care and nurturing of one's marriage is relational vanity.)

IV. **Remember your marriage to keep it holy.** (To keep a marriage holy is to keep it refreshed with plenty of time for play, relaxation, fun-filled adventure. Relationships also need the experience of Sabbath rest.)

V. **Honor your father and your mother ... and your aunts and your uncles and your forebears and your friends.** (By honoring all family and friendship relationships you engage in the simple but necessary recognition that you come from somewhere and some larger tribe, all of which influences your marriage.)

VI. **You shall not harm or hinder the personality traits, dreams and hopes of your beloved.** (What causes one to grow in vision and accomplishment can help the other to grow as well.)

VII. **You shall not commit adultery.** (No contemporizing needed. This is a calling which possess not only spiritual righteousness but also practical guidance.)

13 Lessons I Learned from Falling Off of a Bike

I continue to learn many lessons in the wake of a recent bicycle accident. The following are the most salient:

1. You can't win an argument with asphalt. Things like a bicycle seizing up happen with little or no explanation, and if you fall the asphalt has a distinct advantage.
2. No matter where you are, friends known and unknown friends-to-be will come to help in a time of crisis.
3. In the emergency room, there will always be someone worse off than you. (And then you're provided sufficient time to be profoundly grateful that you did not experience a head, neck or spinal injury.)
4. The wonders of modern medical science never cease. X-rays, MRIs, the capacity to diagnose a physical problem — all of these are miraculous gifts for the lessening of suffering and the furthering of healing.
5. The comforts of medication are nearly indescribable.
6. There is healing in food. Love and healing are interrelated. The dishes generous folks provide contain many nurturing ingredients, love and compassion among them.
7. There is caring in every communication. Cards, e-mails, voice-mails — all bear angelic proclamations.
8. There is exceeding comfort in being with those you love and trusting that everything will be all right.
9. God is as near as the breath we breathe, as consoling as a hug, as liberating as a pain-free morning. And God makes for excellent company in reflective solitude.
10. We are all rich, if we assess the true measures of wealth. We are as rich as our family's love is deep. (And even if family configurations are less than ideal for some folks, there are other riches to celebrate, such as the following.)

11. Health is wealth.
12. Friendship is wealth.
13. A community of care is wealth.

As you can see from the above, it's so very easy for me to say that I'm a very lucky and blessed man.

Things I Know Now That I Wish Knew Then

There are things all of us come to know that we wish we had known before we commenced a venture, or a profession, or a relationship, or a project. We wish we had had a glimpse or a hint or a glimmer of the dangers and challenges that lay ahead. We wish we had had a heads-up about what to watch out for in the adjudicating of important matters of life, in the enactment of a meaningful human journey.

This is so very true for those of us who have been blessed with the opportunity of being of use to people in the *in extremis* moments of their lives, when health is at issue and especially at the end of life.

There are some things I know now — as a pastor and a preacher — that I wish I had known then. I wouldn't have so many hard miles in my soul and body, and, I believe, I would and/or could have been more effective as a minister.

I wish I had known...

- My older peers weren't as stuffy and un-cool as I thought they were.

- How "funereal" (i.e. dead!) some funeral music can be.

- How much a meal, *any* meal — the breaking of bread — can be a sacrament.

- How life-extending machinery would revolutionize the whole essence of end-of-life care.

- How much doctors and nurses need pastoral care in the midst of their work.

- How important it is for clergy to take time away after a funeral.

- How necessary it is for caregivers in end-of-life situations — clergy-chaplains, et. al. — to take ample time for spiritual retreats.

- How little musicians and organists get paid for their essential participation in funeral services.

- That every minister needs a priest or rabbi and every priest needs a minister or rabbi and every rabbi needs a priest or minister. (And we might add imam now to all those scenarios, as well.)
- How very difficult and ultimately rewarding interfaith work is.
- I wish I had known that we clergy have more power than we know. Along with physicians, nurses, and chaplains, we clergy have an immense capacity to educate, to illuminate, to enlighten our peers in other professions. Not only do we have the capacity, we have a duty to do so. Too often clergy are relegated to what I call "the afterwards role" — funeral, burial, etc. — after all the tough stuff — heroic measures or pain management — has been performed. Too often the work we do during a person's illness — prayer, visitation, communion, anointing, simple presence — is seen as ancillary (a side-bar action), as adjacent to the central work of the medical professional. If I had known how necessary and impact-laden a clergy's actions are to a congregant's health, I would have pressed earlier and harder for conversation with doctors and nurses and technicians, so that we all might benefit and so that my congregants (and their patients) could receive more holistic, more effective attention and treatment. And I would have begun, a lot earlier, to invite the entire health care team to the funeral. For the health care and hospital personnel need — spiritually need! — to see their patients deaths not as failures but as completions of an earthly journey.
- I wish I had known then what I know now: a hearty and honestly related expression of ignorance is more welcome and better appreciated than the empty platitudes which sometimes pass for piety. What I mean, straightforwardly here, is that, before we do any more damage, we ought to quit, back off our half-baked notions of the Divine and the Divine's intention for all of us humans. Too often we clergy act and speak as if we know much more than we actually do, in fact, really know. Rarely have I known, in exact detail, what is truly

the will of God. And our people, those souls who have placed their trust in us, know this with a consummate clarity. More often than not our members need most to know we are with them in their struggles and they are not alone, that they are being accompanied by God and by you and me, through the last passage toward their completion upon this globe. That they need and deeply hunger for real information and real comfort and tough honesty, rather than some eked-out, trumped-up presumption about what the will of God is in the midst of a death-dealing cancer at the age of 49.

- I wish I had known more science — in college or graduate school — so I wouldn't have had to play catch-up (usually over some nurse's shoulder) — about blood gasses, blood pressure, and how much blood there is and where it is in the human body. Yes, we all know the "death rattle" sound of troubled breathing when the end is fast approaching in the ICU. But until the last eight years I didn't know how renal failure occurs and at what point the autonomic takes charge and kicks in within the human creature.

- I would have said "I love you" more often, more directly, more clearly to the members of the congregations I have served. We clergy are occasionally stiff and stuffed-to-the-gills with our own personal dignity when we think composure and strength are called for. An aloof detachment, a stern countenance, a stiff upper lip in the midst of dying and death — all these are shames and failures. Conrad Aiken's couplet needs an additional line to make it into a holy tercet of truths —

   Music I heard with you was more than music,
   bread I broke with you was more than bread.
   Tears I shared with you were sheer sacrament.

- We all should be like Jeremiah — free and full in our weeping — with and on behalf of our people.

- I wish I had known then how costly hospital care is and how those costs can psychologically and spiritually oppress those at the end of life and those who remain. I wish I had known just how costly funerals can be and how affordable cremation is and when to suggest one or the other to a family who is strapped financially.

- I wish I had known how personal and pummeled and pulverized and pounded all doctors and nurses are by forces and factors that have nothing to do with the medical arts and sciences in which they were trained and little if anything to do with the performance of their duties. I wish I had known that political correctness and what the Bible calls "avarice" (or greed — one of the seven deadly sins in Catholic tradition) are as much a problem plaguing doctors by those above them as they are for all of us.

- I wish I had known that the emphysema patient still smoking and the cirrhosis patient still drinking and the morbidly obese patient still overeating all signal a communal dysfunctionality, that wherever there is a death-wish being lived out, there's a death-wish script being transmitted to a new generation.

- I wish I had known during the first ten years of my ministerial journey what I have known for the last 10 years — that funeral home directors have an increasingly heavy load of grief-related work on their plates, especially as the culture seems to express an anti-institutional bent when it comes to religion.

- I wish I had known how idolatrous every generation is of their own youth and youthfulness.

- I wish I had known how much we Americans — for at least the last 50 years, but never so rabidly as during the last 15 years — have made an idol of convenience.

- I wish I had known how frequently it will be the case that an estranged, distant relative will intrude in an end-of-life situation with their own narcissistic needs.

- I wish I had known how utterly grace-filled it is to hold the hand of someone who is contemplating their death and then to hold their hand as they are dying, how simply holy it is that their beloved is on one side of them and their rabbi, their pastor, their priest, their imam, is on the other side of them as they are ushered into the next plane of their existence.

ACKNOWLEDGEMENTS

No one produces a book alone. To say otherwise is to commit a forgery and to insult the grace of relationships. So, allow me to avoid both of those fates and say a huge thanks to several people.

For support all through the process and utterly thoughtful steerage to the welcoming embrace at Caroline Street Press, my deepest thanks to Alex Greenwood, wonderful friend and wonderful writer indeed. Thanks, too, to Sonja Shaffer, for typography excellence, and great thanks, as well, to Jason McIntyre, for artistry and deft design finesse.

For the keenest proof-reading skills I've ever been privileged to witness, I offer David Buchmann heartfelt gratitude and admiration.

For the kind readings of Chuck Blaisdell, Rita Nakashima Brock, Brent Schondelmeyer, Bill Tammeus, and the Honorable Emanuel Cleaver II, whose encouragements have made this a better book, blessings upon blessings and a free one on me at the next toasting time.

For the invitation to be a writer for the "Voice of Faith" column in *The Kansas City Star*, and for their extreme welcome and encouragement after I said "Yes," I offer abiding appreciation to Darryl Levings and Elaine Garrison. (Nineteen of those columns are included in the section "20 Questions: A Voice of Faith Answers in the Public Square.")

And for perduring love in life and constant support in writing, I am first and foremost grateful to Priscilla, premier critic, keenest appreciator, and ever and again the best ... always.

ABOUT THE AUTHOR

Robert Lee Hill is a nonfiction writer, poet, and community consultant for non-profit organizations focusing on social justice issues, particularly the increase of community engagement regarding quality education for all students in the Kansas City public schools, empowering citizens through voter registration, and quality health care for all.

Previously he served for more than 30 years at the Community Christian Church (Disciples of Christ) in Kansas City, Missouri, before moving into semi-retirement and being named Minister Emeritus in 2015.

Before his time in Kansas City, he served for four and a half years as Special Projects Director and Co-Director of Project Return, Inc., a non-profit agency working with ex-prisoners and their families in Nashville, Tennessee. Much prior to that, after his first year in college, he was drafted as a Conscientious Objector and spent two transformative years as a Youth and Family Worker at All Peoples Christian Church in South Central Los Angeles, where he would eventually be ordained.

He holds a B.A. degree from Texas Christian University, an M.Div. degree from Vanderbilt University Divinity School, and a D.D. degree from Christian Theological Seminary.

Since 1993, he has been co-host of the renowned Sunday morning radio call-in show, "Religion on the Line," on KCMO-Talk Radio 710 AM/103.7 FM.

He has written or edited nine previous books, including *Life's Too Short for Anything But Love*, *The Color of Sabbath*, and a volume of poems, *Hard to Tell*.

Made in the USA
Columbia, SC
27 December 2019